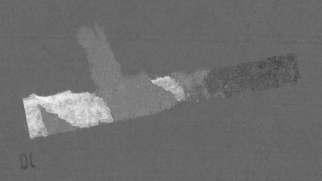

A Craving for Swan

A
Craving
for Swan

ANDREI CODRESCU

 A SANDSTONE BOOK

OHIO STATE UNIVERSITY PRESS : COLUMBUS

Library of Congress Cataloging-in-Publication Data
Codrescu, Andrei, 1946–

A craving for swan.
"A Sandstone book."

I. Title.
PS 3553.03C7   814'.54   86-21878
ISBN 0-8142-0415-5

Contents

———

v

Author's Note

These essays were broadcast on National Public Radio's "All Things Considered" between 1983 and 1985. Some of them appeared in a slightly different form on the Op-Ed page of the *Baltimore Sun* during that same period. The author thanks his kind editors, Art Silverman of ATC and Stephens Broening of the *Sun,* whose incredible patience allowed these rants to be born. Other saintly beings of great comfort to the author in his weekly despair were Margo Hammond, former editor of the *Sun Magazine,* and Alison Chaplin, book editor of the *Sun.* Greater than all of them, however, is Alice Codrescu, my painter wife, whose ideas I have stolen. Paint is slower than words, no matter what they say about worth.

A Craving for Swan

A Craving for Swan

The day after Mardi Gras, in New Orleans, I had a terrible craving for filet of swan. It was nothing I had ever tasted before, God forbid, but something in me called for swan the way Nero called for his violin. Maybe it was the extravagance of the night's revelry, during which a thousand feathered creatures swam by in big wheels of light. Or maybe it was my Transylvanian neck fetish which exalts swans and giraffes, calling for a feverish *rite du printemps*. Maybe it was New Orleans itself, and the bus named Desire, which twice rumbled by leaving me weak-kneed.

I rarely require such recondite satisfactions. I have occasionally lusted and immersed myself in a large Bermuda onion slice lying thickly atop a trembling wheel of head cheese. I have eaten boar and rabbit and snails and frogs' legs, but never elephant or rhino or flamingo. I could never eat parrot or nightingale or owl. Even seafood, with its textural oddities, viscous inconsistencies and insectlike conglomerations, repels me slightly, though I eat it. There is a closed-eyes rapture in the act of swallowing raw oysters *au deux*, the rapture of legend and rumor, no doubt. And in the swallowing of shrimps and the sucking of crabs there resides the ever-so-slight perversity of devouring our origins, a kind of reverse cannibalistic philogeny.

Only the night before, I'd feasted with my friends Philip and Heather on a large brewing pot of hellish sea and land animals gathered by a wild, masked crowd. The drunken, howling mob dived into the liberally spiced caldron with the abandon of guests at a Hollywood pool party. It was my great luck, I thought next day, to have emerged into the sunlight with a relatively sound body. Had all the knowns and the unknowns in the pot decided to tear me apart they could have certainly done so. But like the festival itself, the stew had been good-natured, and amazingly lawful.

But instead of blessing my good fortune, I wandered about craving swan. Oh, dark star! It was therefore with great pleasure that I read in the newspaper about Prince Philip's resignation from the Explorers' Club of New York, because it served hippopotamus and lion steaks at its annual dinner.

The Prince, who is the president of the World Wildlife Fund, said that he was "appalled by the exhibition of bad taste." Of course, had I been the Prince I might have thought twice before abrogating my royal right to eat anything. His ancestors must have eaten the last of many species, including the griffin, the phoenix, and the unicorn. In our day, however, even a prince must control his cravings and eat the commoner's fare.

I took the hint. Had chicken instead.

Stalin

Nobody dies like Stalin did. He didn't just die, he took the world with him. My world, at any rate. I was eight years old when it happened. At school all the kids had been crying and I'd been crying the most. For us, Stalin was that saintly, fatherly figure that smiled from above, surrounded by adoring children. For me, personally, he was father, pure and simple, because I didn't have one of my own. On my little nightstand table I had his portrait and I slept securely under the shadow of his moustache.

Devastated, disbelieving, I came home from school through the back alleys, hiding my tears from everyone. When I got home I saw my stepfather and another man sitting soberly at the kitchen table. Unnoticed, I slipped into the room and hid, too upset to talk.

"I'm glad the sonofabitch is dead," the man said, and my stepfather concurred.

My world was there and then shattered and lost forever. Later, I watched the people cry and tear their hair publicly on the streets, but I somehow knew that it was all a show. They were just using the occasion to grieve, weep, and cry for other sorrows. Stalin was just an excuse to mourn for the world. And I suspected fraud about the whole race of fathers, leaders, and men larger than life.

There are no fathers, I later decided, only moustaches which scatter in the wind, hair by hair, which vanish, disappear, betray, and leave you alone at night.

Chrononaut

When they asked me what I wanted to be when I grew up, I answered: "An explorer!" It was quite the thing for a boy of ten, but imagine being stuck with it. Fashions change but one thing does not: All adults want little boys to be something else besides little boys. Grownups, who are all, with rare exceptions, failures (having never become the things they said they would when they were little boys) ask the little boys that loaded question in order to set the little boys up for failure. In reality, there is only one answer to the question: "What do you want to be when you grow up?"

That answer is: "Not you!"

Anyway, having committed myself, I spent the next thirty years looking for something to explore. Geography was by and large exhausted by the time I got to it. The only earthly explorers left were mining engineers. I didn't want to be a mining engineer. The situation that prevailed and prevails in the heavens wasn't any better: although cosmic exploration is still at the very beginning, it is mostly a military venture, and even as a child I had the good sense to hate the military.

In my twenties I thought that I discovered an alternative: inner space. As vast, if not vaster than outer space, it seemed to stretch for infinity in every direction. It was not long before I realized that much of this inner geography had also been colonized, and that, what's more, I too was colonizing it with my notions, and preparing the way for the mining of its resources by drones of tiny capitalists in search of magic markets.

Only time was left, an explorable dimension made all the more mysterious by its closeness. Federico Garcia Lorca, the Spanish

‥‥‥‥, once said to a friend: "We'll go to town at five o'clock in ‥‥ afternoon, the hour in which the gardens begin to *suffer*." ‥hat a splendid vision of five o'clock, that hour when most people think only of driving home to eat! And how about three o'clock in the P.M., that strange and quiet hour when the whole world is daydreaming?

There is a man, whose name I forget, who wrote somewhere that his life was changed one late evening when, upon leaving his room at Cambridge, he encountered Einstein walking. Einstein asked him what time it was. Momentarily speechless, the man pointed at the tower in the square where Time was writ large. Einstein laughed and the man's life was changed.

It is a fine story, only the man never tells what time it was when this happened. It was 3 P.M., I just know it.

Time's Fingers

A little noticed change has been taking place in our time-world. The advent of digital time has been changing the way we act and think. I believe that it has graduated us to a higher level of anxiety, with greater expectations of efficiency.

The old, round, hand-moved time still retained a certain connection to the natural flow of things, to the roundness of the earth and to the changes of light and seasons. Old, round time was outside ourselves, far enough removed from us so we could ignore it if we so chose.

Not so with digital time, which is a pulse. It beats instead of turning. It imitates the sound of the heart and thus insinuates itself into the body. More and more, we mistake its rhythmic pulse for our own, thus mistaking the demands of the world with our own desires.

Before wrist watches, time used to reside in towers in the centers of towns. At that distance, it could be seen by everybody, but only if they so wished. It took an effort, an actual visit with "time." But then something happened: time first began to live *with* us, and now it is beginning to live *in* us.

I remember what it was like to be a child, immersed in the infinitely stretchable substance of time. For me there was only child time, divided arbitrarily and quite painfully by the edicts of the grownups into Bedtime, Wakeup Time, and Schooltime. But within each of those divisions, Eternity still reigned. Later, of course, they managed to infect me with the anxious demands of clock time. Very soon, all that remained was the anxiety of precision. The swift strokes of the time-piece chopped Eternity to pieces.

Occasionally, I stop long enough to recapture the dimensions of childhood. But not often enough. Like everybody else, I am helpless before the new technologies.

Time is a virus, and it is growing stronger.

When the Flea Wore Shoes

_____

I am a fan of stories but there are fewer and fewer stories in the world. It seems to me that only a few years ago, people told more stories. They grabbed you, they cornered you, they whispered in your ear. I know I did. I often thought that tragedy was having a story to tell and no one to tell it to. But things have changed.

A case can be made against television as a killer of stories. The TV is now our official arbiter of stories, and the stories TV tells are medieval fairy tales interrupted every five minutes by a commercial miracle. In this way TV set storytelling back to the Middle Ages when the supernatural reigned supreme. Realists have gone underground in the wake of TV, and even the gossips among us have a harder time at it. It may well be that real people living in a world they can recognize are quickly going out of fashion.

But maybe it isn't the fault of TV. Maybe TV is only a symptom of our inability to feel at home in the world. To tell a story, you must have a good place to sit and a little time. Time, never much of a commodity in America, has been shrinking at an alarming rate. Composing a story means having time to view your world long enough to take your tale from it. And if you're going to properly tell it, you need not only your own sweet time but the time of your listener.

So what happens to all our unique stories, the stories no one else can tell? We don't tell them and are poorer for it. Our world is deteriorating in direct proportion to our inability to tell our stories. Time, too, gets meaner and shorter when it is measured in money; so though we seem, statistically, to live longer, in fact we live less and die sooner.

Sure, we have plenty of professional storytellers, novelists, and script writers and such, and we pay them well to tell us stories. But are the stories they tell any good? No, they are not, and they wouldn't be even if they were better than they actually are. The paid storytellers could never tell *our* stories. If we accept their stories instead of our own, because we have no time to tell ours, we accept a false view of ourselves as well. Slowly, we become the shallow, brutal, and superstitious creatures in the soap operas and the potboilers. We gradually abandon our world for one made up by people paid to distract us from our lives.

When I was growing up, I spent a summer in the mountains at a sheep farm. In the evenings, the shepherds told stories around the fire. The storytelling began with a series of improbable and wonderful statements, meant to free us from the worries of the day. "When the pear tree made peaches," one man said. "When the flea wore shoes weighing ninety-nine pounds each and still flew into the sky to bring us stories," said another. Once upon a time. Yes, once upon a time there was plenty of time for everything. Time hadn't even begun, it was an idea whose time hadn't come.

I think of those voices from my childhood skillfully weaving us out of time with those magical incantations at the beginning of stories. Couldn't they be of use still? In their way, those formulas were time-machines, and machines, after all, is what we're supposed to be so good at.

Bear with Me

I told my son Tristan this story: "In a forest far away, a bear ate a certain mushroom and, lo and behold, he was transformed into a school child. Finding himself in a regular school unable to convince anyone that he is really a bear not a child, he takes to the road and wanders forlorn. When he meets another child on the road, he tells him: 'I'm a bear!' To his great surprise, the fellow traveler answers him: '*I'm* a bear!' It turns out that something similar had befallen this bear-child too. The two of them team up and soon they meet another child. 'I'm a bear! I'm a bear! I'm a bear!' they confess, and a third bear-child joins them. To make a long story short, they are joined by seven more bear-children wandering the roads in search of their lost bear-hood and then they meet another child. They joyfully greet him with: 'I'm a bear! I'm a bear! I'm a bear! I'm a bear! I'm a bear! I'm a bear! I'm a bear! I'm a bear! I'm a bear! I'm a bear!,' to which the newcomer says: 'I'm a bird!' Nevertheless, he joins up, and soon the army arrives at the edge of the forest . . ."

I won't tell you all the rest of what happened. If you want to know, you have to ask Tristan. But this much suffices for what I have been thinking about all these many days and more, namely, that bears are the very few successful survivors of the rich bestiary that once populated our fables and yarns. Maybe it is because bears have been humanized to the point where very little bear survives in them. There isn't much mouse in Mickey, so maybe bears bear only a faint resemblance to the animal bearing that name. But I refuse to believe that! I like to think that in spite of everything, a little bear survives in our fabulous bears.

In a story called "Days of Leave-Taking" by the Soviet writer Andrei Bitov, the narrator takes his daughter to the zoo. At the bear's cage, looking at the animal who is mechanically opening his mouth for candy, the man has a staggering realization. He realizes that the bear is mad. He realizes that the bear no longer exists. "I am convinced," he says, "that in its gaze there was precisely the madness of the final survivor. It may have been that the bear had given up on living any longer: not that this particular bear (individually) had given up—but that in him bear in general had given up; that *in him* there no longer remained the vital energy *to be bear*."

Leaving aside the possible allusion linking the Soviet bear with this bear, the thought is, in itself, utterly chilling. What if, in addition to our killing them, the animals are going crazy? Indeed, Bitov says: "Isn't it strange that we make more and more books with fairy tales and pictures about wild rabbits and wolves and foxes, and we still make fish and reindeer and teddy bears out of rubber and plastic and stuffing and realize less and less what it is we are doing. Our children already live in a world where there are thousands of times more toy animals than there are animal animals."

On the cover of *The Three Bears* in the Little Golden Book edition, I behold a mischievous nymphette being looked over with varying degrees of solicitude by a greedy little bear dressed in *spielhosen,* a mother bear who looks like Edith in "All in the Family," and a giant daddy bear with his hands behind his back and a carpenter's apron around his formidable waist. And in looking at them, the meaning of my little story comes suddenly to me: If there are no more bears left in the forest, surely there must be some among us, disguised as humans. Where could all that bearness go if not in *us* who so delight in it? It is possible that at any given time, in any given gathering, a number of us are bears. And birds. And mice.

I am bird-bear.

Eternal Youth

There is a man in Florida who is 350 years old and he is still in elementary school. None of his classmates suspect anything. For all his great age, this very old student still can't read very well. He claims that the secret of his extraordinary longevity and his youthful good looks is precisely this ignorance.

The hundreds of thousand-year-old people in the Caucasus, the Himalayas, and the Carpathians arrive at great ages also, with the aid of daily doses of yogurt, cigarettes, vodka, and dubious birth records. Here, as in the case of the Floridian, ignorance (of legal and medical facts) appears to be the cause of long life.

Every year in the Soviet Union and in Sikkim, two thousand-year-old men are presented simultaneously to the press. With the exception of their eyelashes, which reach to the ground, they are in very good shape. Each of them begins the day with a jog up an unclimbable crag, a pint of vodka, a gallon of fermented yak milk, a jar of hot pickles, and a pack of handrolled cigarettes. After breakfast, thirteen hours straight of back-breaking work follow. The two men are brothers. They haven't seen each other since the Crusades, but they hope to, soon, when they get the time. They have started walking toward each other several times (they often have the same urge simultaneously), but after several hundred miles they became entangled in the jungle of modern road signs, which they were unable to read, and turned back. They keep track of their descendants with a bone abacus but they have been promised a computer. Of course, they are extremely virile, and have been known to pinch women reporters.

Studies of eternal youth are at an infantile stage, but it appears that ignorance is extremely helpful. Learning how to read had proved fatal in several cases. An old mountain woman in Peru was forced to take a class and faded visibly the very next day. In other cases, literacy is not so dramatically responsible for the decline but the signs are unmistakable. An old man in the Mississippi Delta reputed to be 329 years old was taught to read, whereupon he read a single issue of a newspaper and decayed rapidly. There are no studies yet on the link between reading the newspaper and aging. It is my guess that people who read the newspaper every day die sooner, quicker, and more definitively.

There is a growing conviction in eternal youth studies that literacy is a virus. The near-universal conviction that we must know how to read hides the fact that after we learn we have our brains slowly replaced by what other people say, a condition that cannot, in the end, be beneficial. The time spent reading is withdrawn as well from our total vitality account. Sucked dry by other people's thoughts, and time-depleted, we fulfill the statistics. (After we read them.)

An interesting development in cancer research throws a new light on the aging process as well. According to Dr. Eliade, the original purpose of the cancer cell was to create new organs in order to renew the body, so that we may live forever. But something happened and, instead of stopping when the organs had been renewed, the growth went on to kill. Dr. Eliade calls this not knowing when to stop, "ontological amnesia." Cancer forgot. In other words, it became absentminded, it got lost in trivia, it probably started reading the newspapers.

The doctor speculates that it might be possible to teach cancer to remember, to make it "ontologically present," to awaken it to its true purpose. Water may turn the trick. Yes, water, a simple glass of water from a special place. Of course, we didn't need medical science to tell us. People's folklore, before they learned to read, is full of stories about the Fountain of Youth, the River of Life, the Spring of Happiness. There is the one Ponce de

León found in Florida. There are several in the high Urals and Himalayan mountain chains. There is one in Rockefeller Plaza in New York.

Living to a ripe old age of, let's say, five hundred through the graces of a simple combination of cancer and magic water (a combination, that is, of forgetfulness and remembering) is entirely feasible. But few literate people would be willing to believe this. They would rather go in for lamb fetus injections, total skin transplants, hormone treatments, desperate diets, and illustrated magazines.

A woman of a mere three hundred, Dr. Ana Salajan, well known for her invention of the famous and still-banned (except in Florida) drug Gerovital, said recently that people would be amazed to find out how easy it is to stop the aging process. But she stopped short of saying it. In Romania, where her offices are located, there are several fountains of youth and a great number of illiterate peasants. Good water and no books, is what she could have added.

I offer these thoughts strictly for the benefit of my generation, that bulge in the middle of the century, known affectionately as the "baby boom." They are beginning to worry about when to go into deep freeze and how to stay young forever, and so they are reading all they can about it. Personally, I don't really care. Being from Romania makes you automatically a thousand years older than everybody.

No Now Now

Gertrude Stein said about Oakland that "there is no there there." Had she been living now she would have said that "there is no now now." At least that's what I say: there is no now now.

Nowness is a subtle intoxication, a spirit perhaps, that infuses the world with a sense of magic. People and objects are enhanced by nowness, so that they appear both beautiful and glowing. It is also an optimum of attention: the eyes do not glide carelessly over what they see: they are riveted to what comes into them.

Perhaps what I am describing is only the exhiliration of youth, adolescence to be exact, a state of physiological newness. But no, it wouldn't do to confuse now with new. Or perhaps only in the sense that there is more now in the new.

Maybe it is a seasonal thing: there is always now in the spring, and no now in the winter.

It may even be a multi-thing: there may be whole slews of now. A now of the social body, when suddenly people become conscious of injustice and deceit, and they stir angrily to action. There might be a now of science, when suddenly a thousand discoveries are made, and everyone feels like they're walking on air. There surely is a now of the arts, when people begin talking in multi-colored bubbles like cartoon characters, and beauty is so obvious only executioners don't see it.

Nowness may be a surplus of vital substance, a spillage of the Mysterium. It may be a well-regulated quantity that sometimes overflows, the way the keepers of dams and reservoirs sometimes open them to let out the excess rain.

Whatever it is, we have always tried to locate it and drink from it.

Every tribe has fairy tales about the magic water of life and of youth. These are the waters of now, for which an eternal search has been organized by human beings since before history. In fact, history is only the string of incidents incurred during the search.

Whatever it is, there isn't much now now, and I'm going on the road.

Immortality

Most people don't have a big craving for immortality. They
don't have the appetite of John Keats, for instance, who wanted
to "glean" all "his teeming brain" before he "ceased to be." Most
people's brains don't teem, unless ravaged by fever. For most, a
few markers suffise: a clipping from the local paper noting their
presence at the firemen's ball, a notice in the company news-
letter, a favorable graffito on a familiar wall. Their picture in the
year book is what most people use to assure themselves that
their passing through was noted and inscribed. The yearbook
picture doesn't just record: it also places one in the midst of
one's contemporaries, it reassures one of having belonged in a
certain place at a specific time.

Children, of course, are everyone's bid for continuance. They
are solid and visible, unlike the vague gleanings of the brain.

And then there are the Napoleons among us. For inexplicable
reasons they turn the world upside down seeking to plant
their image everywhere. Napoleon, no less than Keats, meant to
insure for himself a kind of immortality that did not fade with a
yellow scrap of paper. But for every successful suitor of lasting
fame, there are millions who fail. Some of the failures are clever
though, inserting themselves like time bombs into the body of
the future, there to explode when everyone least expects it. One
such person was the possessor of the original script of *Tristan
and Isolde,* a manuscript so rare it would have insured one of
eternal life just to be known as its *copier.* What Hans Magnus
Bruckenthal did, however, was to mail a page of this script to
each of his many correspondents around the world. One by one,
the priceless pages began showing up many years after his death,
prompting wild speculation among the collectors. The hunt that

followed, for the missing pages, achieved what Hans Magnus meant them to in the first place: they gathered together a picture of Hans himself, who emerged from those letters quite an interesting man, even memorable perhaps. Having piggybacked his way to immortality on the back of Tristan and Isolde, he assured his own. His timer was set to explode years after everyone had forgotten his contemporaries.

The craving for immortality is a curse, but also a sweet poison. Is anyone truly free of it? I doubt it. It's probably a matter of scale, and appetite.

Fashion Peasants

Thank God leg warmers are out. I uttered a sigh of relief when wooden clogs bit the dust, too. I will be ecstatic when stone-washed jeans go the way of all fads. There is something about the unfinished peasant look that gets on my nerves. From sheepskins turned inside out to bark shoes, the fashion industry has been raiding the dwindling peasants of the world.

Too bad that the only thing it took from them was the fur on their backs and the leggings from their calves. Peasants have stories that go with those clothes. Leggings, for instance, are wraparound books, containing instructions for dealing with mean winds and rabid dogs. Wood shoes should be turned upside down at night so that roots won't grow from them. Sheepskins are often supposed to have a life apart, as manifested in their dancing around when nobody's looking. And stone-washed things are washed at the river rhythmically, the thump of the stones being song and signal.

What happens when we unthinkingly take over these things is that we become psychically disturbed. Like the people in California who live under the redwoods although the Indians warned them about the souls of the dead contained in those trees, we become slowly discombobulated by appropriation without narration.

In Mexico City, for instance, all the hookers were wearing leg warmers last year. There was no danger of confusing them with aerobic dancers. Everyone else wore them around their ankles. Somewhere in the Andes, peasants were rolling with laughter. In my mind, I can still hear the clip-clop of wooden shoes across the bare floors of the mid-seventies. The smell of wet sheepskins is likewise forever in my nostrils. Sad to say that if I met a real peasant today I would think of him or her as an anthology of fashion.

I wouldn't know what it was.

The End of the Person

When the perennial question of what to wear came up, I noticed
that I didn't much care. I just threw on a leather jacket over a
T-shirt and kept my professor pants on. My wife put on some
kind of Indian skirt and then an old velvet dress on top of that,
with a short padded Army jacket over that, and combat boots
for good measure. The art opening we went to was attended
mostly by folks who looked so instantly familiar I immediately
forgot what they were wearing. The one exception was a woman
in a leather miniskirt with fake Barbie hair and spiked hi-heeled
shoes. And I only remember her because she reminded me
vaguely of sex. At the bar we went to after the opening, there
were semi-punks drinking champagne, and guys in suits drinking
whiskey. The punks were probably businessmen who'd taken off
their suits, and the businessmen were probably punks who'd put
them on. Later we went to another place, a nightclub where you
had to wait in line. A girl in back of us said to her girlfriend:
"I'm wearing everything I got. I came here with a suitcase, and
I'm wearing everything in it." She looked perfectly normal to
me. A little of this and a little of that. That's just it, I thought to
myself. Not so long ago, people really agonized when they went
out. It wasn't just a matter of clothes: they had to decide *who*
they wanted to be. There was a time there in the seventies when
everybody worried about their persona: they wouldn't go out if
they couldn't project a certain image, be some *thing*. Before
that, in let's say, the sixties, there were only two kinds of folk,
straight and hip. You dressed like one or the other. Way back in
the fifties, everybody was square. You wore whatever everybody
else did. Before that, in prehistory, people dressed like what they
really were. Peasants dressed like peasants. Soldiers like soldiers.

Judges like judges. Bums like bums. But we've come to the end of history: we are all one thing today: bored humans: it doesn't matter what we wear, it doesn't even matter who we are. We're back to the basics.

Ask the Warm Furrier

My greatest sorrow is that I don't have a tail, a pair of wings, and a thick, warm coat of fur. I keenly envy the animals theirs.

I spend hours daydreaming of a limber, long tail I could curl around the back of the seat on the bus or around a telephone pole while I'm waiting for one.

Wings, of course, I don't have to explain. A large, mottled pair of wings I can wrap myself in as I sit at the top of the World Trade Center, surveying the winds: ah, can you think of anything better?

And last but not least, I would appreciate a few thickly matted inches of fur covering my entire body with the exception of my eyes. An ideal being to me is a sort of winged wolfman with a comet tail. I can't believe that evolution would do anything as stupid as to drop our tail, wings, and fur. That had to be punishment for something. The whole thing is fishy.

Wings and tail are, alas, out of our reach. (I don't go in for phony imitations like hang-gliding and kite-flying which only expose you to the ridicule of the birds). Fur, however, is another matter.

People have been slipping into animal skins as soon as they were able to kill them. History has been insufficiently studied from the point of view of the fur trade. The fur trade is not, as often believed, part of the general history of trade. It is not on a par with other commodities.

Catherine the Great's sailors came all the way to California for fur. The West was settled partly by mountains of pelts piled high in front of trading posts. Animals have been destroyed for fur more often than for meat. Magic furs haunt the myths of all people. Argonauts and astronauts share equally the purpose of finding a golden fleece. (NASA may tell you differently but don't believe them: The space program is a secret quest for the fur of space creatures.)

All of history is a search for the softest, thickest wrap, as well as the prettiest. Money and its abstractions are a smoke screen in the face of the real economy of the planet, which is based on a huge desire for fur.

We have gone to great lengths to deny our kinship with animals (such as killing them) while our secret motive all this time has been our envy of them, the impossible sadness of our plucked, boiled-looking bodies.

So let us rejoice in the fact that it is winter, thank God, and a time to look as much like an animal as possible. This time of the year I do not envy Hawaiians, Jamaicans, and Cubans. Let them sweat in their pitiful cottons! We, great, furry beasts, lurch forward in the cold making big groans and loud thumps!

My life has been a long succession of coats. There is a picture of me at four, wearing a dog-collar jacket with obvious satisfaction and a sort of tongue-lolling expression on my face. I was trying, I'm sure, to look like a dog. Behind me is my mother, unaware of that intention, which she would have promptly censured, wrapped in a waist-length raccoon coat, with a funny, dewy-eyed expression on *her* face. But she, I believe, is not trying to look like a raccoon but rather like Greta Garbo.

Later, I appear on the elementary school scene in a long raincoat with snap-in fake fur. It was an unhappy time in my life: I couldn't decide, the whole four years, what animal I was, and it made me shy, withdrawn, and cranky.

Things started looking up with a dashing sheepskin with red embroidery, a gentle, warm coat made doubly pleasant by the fact that sheep hand over their fur voluntarily. I skidded through early adolescence in this getup, an eminently agreeable young man.

My great melancholy youth began with a black peacoat without any fur. The discontent I felt with the world and myself at that time had to do with the debilitating and severe absence of fur anywhere near my body. Even today, when things go badly, I put on a black peacoat to experience my rage to its depths.

Since then I have had a succession of coats, each of which is a story. But I must stop now: I'm going to see my furrier.

The Bourgeois Birds

<hr />

Like big, black birds, thousands of umbrellas descended on me shortly after I met my wife at the "Lost & Found" counter of the university. At first, I was shy. I noticed her sitting there, reading a book, blonde and dazzling, surrounded by the enormous umbrella trees. The shelves, which started at her feet, climbed into the clouds, stacked full of furled umbrellas. We left the place in the rain carrying a blue umbrella because she believed that black umbrellas made the world gloomy like those dismal English funerals in the movies. During the next rain, we took a yellow umbrella and then a plastic white umbrella. But then, it kept raining and only black umbrellas remained in the little office. Nobody ever came to claim them, and for the next few months we floated out of the campus under those black domes, sealed for all the world like astronauts because we were in love.

Of all the objects ever adopted by Western man, the umbrella is the most curious. Absurd, patently bourgeois, and utterly bizarre, the umbrella stands in the modern psyche like the ancient bird of Roc which was said to carry whole houses in its claws. Seen from the rooftop of an apartment building, the creatures wrapped in umbrellas below look like failed flight machines, endlessly trying to rise. A city in the rain is a melancholy sight: thousands of sad, wet bubbles scurry to dry, warm islands rumored to exist somewhere. Furled, the umbrella is a walking stick curled like a question mark, casting doubt and confusion. Unfurled, it is the sail of a walking boat going nowhere.

The Dadaists, who invented modern art, noticed the umbrella right from the beginning. "Dada," they said, "is the chance meeting of an umbrella and a sewing machine on an operating table." Charlie Chaplin, in fact, epitomized the sadness of our time with his faithful umbrella. It can be said that our century began with Chaplin's furled umbrella and could end under the sign of America's unfurled atomic umbrella. But I won't say anything like that. Once you start making symbols out of this pathetic object, there is no telling where you might end up.

It is much more pleasant to think, for example, how much bloodshed might have been avoided if Cortes's soldiers, pouring on horseback out of his ships, would have been carrying umbrellas instead of swords. Montezuma's warriors, already convinced that the six-legged creatures were gods, would have ceased hostilities entirely, coming, instead, out of the rain to hide under the Spanish umbrellas. America would have been the continent of peace and dry contentment.

Of course, umbrellas aren't entirely harmless. The highest point of technical sophistication having been reached by the Bulgarian Secret Service, we have the amusing (but deadly, alas) spectacle of short, squat Communist agents poking people with the tips of their umbrellas in the London subways. These people fall over, the poisoned tips retract, and the short, squat men retire into bathrooms to reload. These umbrellas, developed over years of secret research, are, of course, black.

Other evil has been attributed to the umbrella. Everyone knows that cataclysm awaits whoever is foolish enough to open an umbrella in the house. As with a broken mirror, seven years of bad luck and rainy weather are sure to follow. I've heard of a case where a whole lot of people opened umbrellas indoors one day and *the whole city* suffered a long deluge. That city is Detroit and the natives are still drying out. I know. I was there.

In China and Japan the umbrella is high art. Made out of silk, painted with birds or snowy mountains, the object transcended its utilitarian function long ago to become a thing of beauty like a screen or a fan. But in our Western world, alas, all such attempts have failed. Doomed to the ridiculous by something as subtle as wind and as brutal as rain (or vice versa), the umbrella never rose from its dour middle-class mold to inspire us to poetry. But for the shelter it once offered the young lovers from "Lost & Found," I am grateful. Think kindly of this maligned bubble when next you grip it.

Animals in the Rain

The animals like to stand in the rain. It pours roundly on all
sides of the ostriches: their eyes are closed, their elevated beings
soothed in every feather. The giraffes stand so still you can hear
rivulets of water rushing down their vertiginous necks. The
ducks, of course, go bananas: they whir like mini-helicopters
around the pond and the fish jump into their beaks. The water
pouring down the faces of the banana leaves collects in pools
which the smaller birds ravage ferociously. But I like best the
way the alligators take it. They make themselves soft like the
mud they originally crawled from and stretch so long and so far
you mistake them for the logs everyone forever mistakes for
alligators. Tropical rain is, of course, a God. From it came these
alligators, and certainly these dozens of turtles swimming necks
outstretched everywhere you care to look.

Only the people are afraid of the rain. Bunched up under the
patio roof of the café, they hold on to soggy hotdogs and plastic
cups like rafts of junk in the debauched water drama surrounding them. A priest dressed in black stands at the edge of the
patio with his black umbrella half-open, clearly caught in the
teeth of a dilemma: should he go or should he stay. These are
big drops of rain, at least as big as the tears the statues of the
saints cry on certain blessed days. Should he dare walk through
the weeping of the sky or should he stay dry like everyone else?
Poised there, on the edge, between human shelter and animal
delight, he seems a picture of all our dilemmas.

But then—out among the animals, perfectly exposed under
the heavens, stepping lightly, dancing almost, here come two
lovers, a boy and a girl, arms around each others' wet T-shirted
midriffs, singing "Singing in the Rain," with a French accent.

And for a moment, the ducks, giraffes, and alligators all splash at the same time. And the priest, his mind all made up now, steps right up into a puddle.

August

August is a dramatic month. Humidity is a form of madness. Writing is a form of suicide. The temptation to talk like this, in short clips, is overwhelming. Short sentences are like raindrops: loud, splashy, and desirable.

August, the most complacent month. Laziness, humidity, and utter lack of thought are its chief characteristics. Sluggish and indolent, we drag our bodies through its sweaty middle like primeval crawlers.

I saw a guy, prostrate from heat, staring at an empty parking lot downtown. "There are more leaves on the trees this year," he said. I looked at the expanse of steaming cement before us and agreed. That was an August encounter and that man an August character. An ambassador of Humidity. The reason why so many people die in August is that nobody is really awake. All Death has to do is pluck the unalert from the planet like overripe peaches.

If you are poor and hot like me, one way to escape August is to visit showrooms. Not only are they airconditioned, they are educational. I went to an IBM computer showplace and a dear lady paraded me before the friendly pastels of a thousand keyboards. It was like ice cream.

Looking over the Augusts of my life, I find all sorts of delirious phenomena. Once I was mugged in a hallway. I was too irritated by the heat to pay. I screamed at the guy and he only took half the money. A few years ago, my wife produced a wonderful calendar full of useful and wonderful facts, as well as the birthdays of all our friends. I tried to talk her into leaving August out. When she wouldn't listen, I went through her files and had several people I didn't like moved to August. She caught me. I pleaded humidity. I don't think she's forgiven me yet.

I Am Not in Paris

Every spring I get a disease called "I am not in Paris." It's a bad affliction. It starts with images of walking down Boulevard Pasteur to Saint Germain-de-Prés, and it reaches its critical stage with briskly walking and bewildered French girls caught between fashion and weather. It's too cold for what they are wearing, but it's officially spring so they are wearing it. Their goosebumps form a great parachute from which I bail out into an indistinct happiness. The disease runs its course through melancholy and sweet visions of the great Parisian cemeteries clothed in tender green leaves, where sleep my literary heroes.

"Don't you suppose," my friend Nadia said, "that if you were in Paris you might get the disease called 'I am not in Baltimore'?" I suppose, but I doubt it. My friend Nadia is an eminently sensible person. She believes you shouldn't get diseases you could avoid. But according to that kind of logic, you shouldn't be anywhere. They've proven that the air itself is lethal.

But she is not altogether wrong. Baltimore is lovely in the spring. There are sweet green things everywhere, and the earth and buildings breathe a kind of ancient sigh. The gardens explode, and on North Charles Street the artists are getting suntans. And, of course, they don't have baseball in Paris. The kids there kick things with their feet, but unless the ball hits a window and a classic shrew of a concierge starts pouring boiling water on the pedestrians, it's nothing to get excited about.

And yet—and yet there is something in Paris that loosens the binds of winter like no place else. And the disease runs its sweet course.

When the Worlds Open

There is a story they tell where I come from. At the stroke of midnight on a midsummer night, the earth, the sky, and the underworld are joined. They open into one another, and it is possible, for a brief second, to travel between worlds. Intrepid travelers, heroes of magic tales, and even plain and bewildered humans have been known to dash between heaven and hell. Return has been problematic, and only after great trials, at the end of another year, during the same magic night, were they able to do so.

Some say that Stonehenge and perhaps the Egyptian and Mayan pyramids are flying machines, places that mark the spot where worlds join. These great star machines become fully functional on the solstice, permitting some to leave and others to return. There are many other places designated by legend as being entryways to other worlds. In any case, the din of broom flyers and magnetized dancing nudes fills those neighborhoods.

Personally, the night of the solstice fills me with dread. I don't like the sound of the German word *Walpurgisnacht* because a vague smell of burning wafts from it. You may call that genetic memory but it might not be all that far back. And then there is the fact that this is the shortest night of the year, a concentrated island of darkness in the middle of an immense day. Having been born on the longest night of the year, in winter, I resent the loss of so much night to the corrosion of daylight. I like my nights long and full and roomy. There is something of the panic of the end of the world in the frantic activity inside so brief a time of darkness.

Eschatology, which is the science of the end, rules the summer solstice because it signals the coming of darkness. The winter solstice, on the other hand, signifies rebirth even in the midst of the longest night.

But maybe this is just sour grapes because I haven't been invited to do any broom flying this year.

Give 'Em Enough Rope

Everything in the universe is made out of strings. So say the proponents of the latest theory to take physics by storm. All the basic particles of which the universe is made are tiny strings, instead of points, as previously assumed. Physicists are attracted to the Superstring Theory because of its "beautiful mathematical structure." I am attracted to it because I knew it all along.

In the first place, I have seen these strings. They are luminous, and if you pull them you can watch the universe change. There are several kinds of strings, and many kinds of string pulling. One kind of string connects all living things. One of the major, if little known, dangers of television is that it snips the luminous strings that connect living things to one another. The order of strings that connects TVs to one another is more primitive. The major activity of our tangled universe is the pulling of strings. The growth of a human being can be measured simply by whether it "knows the ropes." If it does, it's an adult. The major adult question is "Who's pulling the strings?" An adult who knows the ropes and who pulls the strings is a super-adult. The physicists see in the string theory the best hope for a unified theory accounting for all the particles of nature and the forces that control them, including gravity. This would be a kind of super-adult theory, cognizant of string-pulling at all levels.

Previous theory, namely, that the universe is made out of points, was naive. You can make all the points you want, they will amount to nothing if you don't know the ropes. And who's pulling the strings. The only problem I foresee is that another theory may be waiting in the wings, namely, that the universe is made entirely of tiny hammers and sickles. I saw those too, another time.

Meanwhile, watch the ball of yarn. Penelope and Ariadne keep us spinning.

Sad Dish

It was vacation time at my in-laws' Michigan farm, and they'd scheduled entertainment for us. We took a long dirt road to nowhere, past little old farmhouses standing alone under trembling satellite dishes searching the heavens for television. I could imagine them late at night, under the stars, stretched like fishing nets in search of baseball from Japan or nymphs from Chicago.

The long dirt road went past it and ended at a hand-scrawled sign that said: MOVIE OUTPOST. Underneath, a smaller hand had scrawled: *Fireworks*. Behind the roughly hewn counter of the shack, a young Daisy Mae dispensed video discs and tapes to a knotty group of tabbaki-chawing farmers. "I'll have that thar *Star Wars,* and er, that *Bloody Mama* and *Popsicle Girls* . . ."

On the way back, I mused on the strangeness of global earth and wondered just what all this remote-control urban imagery was doing in the true remoteness of this country. Was there anything in this geography physically and culturally hospitable to it? I tended to doubt it, and missed, in my nostalgic old way, all the lost conversations, the never woven weavings, the never told tales. In their stead stood this electronic protection against the land and the sky, broadcast anonymously from Frankenstein's huge chamber in the Nowhere.

If the Russians want to figure out why the American worker will never make a revolution they should meet S., my in-laws' neighbor. He lives on an eighty-acre farm but he's not a farmer. He can't afford to be. He works instead in a factory forty miles from the place. He has a dish satellite, two VCRs, a Zenith color TV and eight hundred videotapes. If S. ever loses his job, he won't make a revolution. He'll make repairs. And he'll watch, watch, watch.

The No Video Planet

Who says miracles don't happen anymore?

I was reaching for a metaphor in class the other day, to make my point clear, and I had a moment of sudden panic. It was as if all common language between myself and the thirty-three young souls in front of me had vanished. I looked at the girl with the semipunk do and the ankle bracelets, and I didn't know how to make myself understood to her. Nor could I make the three fraternity boys in the back get my meaning. How go beyond their smiling crewcuts to the crux of the simple point I was making? A metaphor was urgently needed, but all I had in stock was literary material. That clearly wouldn't do. There was music, of course, always music, but my music was not the punkette's, and not the preps'. There were movies, but here too there stretched a gulf of missed summer releases. But worst of all, I knew that the only language they *did* have in common was not mine. They had TV and MTV and I haven't had a TV in half a year, and everything about it, not just the names of the faces on it, has left my mind.

I felt once again the way I did when I literally spoke another language and could not make myself understood in English. I stood fumbling in the dark before the thirty-three expectant video natives. The knobs were out of reach. The punkette shifted uneasily in her viewing booth and I allowed that horror of horrors, silence, to occur. In America there is only one fear greater than the fear of having your TV taken away, the Fear of Silence. We are so thoroughly drenched in noise that our voices have taken on the metallic eeriness of speaking machines. When the sound stops, the world ends. But even then, as long as the images go on, there is still hope. But when both sound and images are off, an abysmal and apocalyptic horror sets in.

This was beginning to happen now, to the enormous discomfort of everyone present, when there was a crashing sound and the door flew open, revealing a large man standing there with a TV on wheels. His T-shirt said Audio-Visual Department. Everyone breathed a sigh of relief.

Not me. I hadn't ordered any such thing.

The Object of Fire

Our friends had a fire over Christmas. It was an unfortunate event but, luckily, they were out at the time. When they sat down to figure out what had been damaged and what had escaped, they found that everything old had escaped and everything new had melted. For instance, ceramics, brass, and, strangely, even wood, were undamaged. On the other hand, clocks, radios, stereos, records, and telephones became grotesque lumps of matter.

Think about our materials. In the Stone Age, the few objects a human possessed must have been of staggering duration: a stone axe, an animal skin, a catapult, a leather-and-bone mask. In a fire, these things would have given off the hard sound of resistance. The sound of that age must have been the dense thud of stones struck together, a sound of duration and triumph. The few thoughts in the mind of Stone Age Man must likewise have been hard, durable, central, permanent.

The Iron and Bronze Ages brought a certain hollowness with them. Metal striking metal. The clanking of weapons, the jingle of ornaments. The objects of that time were prey only to rust. Rust is the work of time, so it must have been then that the idea of Time appeared. The solid thoughts of Neolithic Man became suddenly fragile, exposed to time, shaken from duration.

The Age of Linens, Silks, Satins, but above all, Sails, brought with it a vast inflation of thought. The typical sound of this age was the rustling of curtains, the flapping of linen on clotheslines, the whisper of petticoats, the creaking of ships going places, the flight of ideas. The Age of Sails was the last time a certain balance between man and objects was still possible. It was the last age when it was possible to know everything. It is also the time when whatever was left of the thoughts of Stone Age Man sank under and disappeared. Yeats said about this: "Things fall apart; the centre does not hold."

The Age of Plastics in which we live has no sound. The sad, shriveling buzz of melting plastic is barely audible and unremarkable. The main feature of our age is the extraordinary quantity of things we must keep track of. How think at all with so much to count?

Most of all, our friends lamented the loss of their Apple II computer, which, they said, helped them keep track of everything. It was a thing that added up all their things. Maybe, I thought, remembering Yeats again, Apple II is causing the Second Fall.

Great Balls of Fire

I lived for some time in a town that burned down every winter. It was a pretty place, nestled against hills, on the side of a river, and the hundreds of smoking chimneys must have made a pretty picture for the tourist. Although piped gas was available, most people preferred their wood stoves and fireplaces. Wood stoves came in a bewildering variety and, in the midst of an energy crisis, they were an attractive alternative.

The cheapest one you could buy, and the first one we had, was made by the next door neighbor, a car mechanic, who drilled a hole at the top of a fifty-gallon oil drum and cut a door in the lid. You then set this contraption in the middle of your living room on three tin legs on a bed of eight bricks and, after attaching a length of pipe to the top and making it go outside through the nearest wall, you fed it all your burnables.

The thing made an infernal amount of instant heat: Flames roared in it as the drum shook and rolled. There was no getting next to it until the fire died down, which defeated its purpose: It was too hot a few feet away and too cold any farther out. So you hopped in and out of the circle of heat, warm one minute, freezing the next.

A coal stove followed the oil drum, a heavy cast-iron object about a hundred years old which, I am sure, had given hundreds of people black lung and would have kept doing it if I had been able to figure out how to get it started. I arranged the coals intricately, with bits of paper and dry twigs, poured whole cans of lighter fluid over it and dropped in all the matches in the house. Like an old dog, it must have been used to certain rituals I couldn't fathom. It remained cold throughout the winter, as the volunteer fire department worked overtime all around us.

I have inherited a tiny bit of the enormous fear of fire that runs in my family. My mother is mortally afraid of it, a fear she inherited from her mother, who inherited it from hers. In my mother's most vivid nightmares, misfortunes work up gradually through floods and earthquakes to the supreme unleashing of flame. In this, she follows unknowingly the destruction myths of many people, including the Hopis, an American Indian tribe who believe that the first world of humans was destroyed by Flood, the second by Earthquakes, and the third by Fire. But in my mother's, as in my grandmother's case, something more recent than myth is mixed up in the fear: They have both seen war from very close up. A long tongue of flame runs through the Eastern European past they share. Memories of pogroms, the burning of towns, bombs falling. Very little of that filtered down to me, and mostly in the form of mumbled injunctions in my childhood, not to "stare at the fire too long . . ."

But I like staring at the fire. A nice fire, mind you, firmly enclosed in a sturdy fireplace with a glass door. I'm not crazy about burning buildings like most people and, of all the dark impulses of the soul, arson is the one I understand the least. But quiet, gentle flames on a November evening, well, there is something both ancient and comforting about it.

If this was the world's first television, I can see why it's still the best. For one thing, the shows aren't boring. You can watch a Paleolithic game show where a dinosaur asks of a monkey: "What percentage of pterodactyls think the ice age will come?" and before the monkey can answer, the program has changed to a meditation on modern painting. There are no commercials and the images go on as long as your imagination.

Conversation, which used to be an art and is now a groaning swamp of platitudes, revives briefly with a good fire. Flames seem to give the words the little extra light they need to mean something. By contrast, TV is nothing but noise and contrived tinsel. Watching just now the reflection of the flames on the cold television screen, I had the oddest sensation that the TV set was afraid. Afraid perhaps of the enormous imagination it had replaced? Or afraid simply that one of those red tongues might reach out to lick it? It is almost too much trying to resist the vision of the burning TV. And I realize that even I, with my inherited fear, can do little against the passion in this ancient companion of mankind.

The Telephone

I've had it with the telephone. This impertinent object, with its abominable timing, rings only in midst of your most intimate moments. The telephone is to tenderness what a hammer is to an egg. It has regard neither for you nor for your silences. It has, in fact, succeeded in making us jumpy and fearful, rarely out of reach of its cord, that leash by which we stand attached to the impersonal meanness out there.

The worst things I have ever heard—such as the death of a friend—have come to me via the telephone. I find myself looking at it in superstitious awe as it stands perched there, seeming to demand human sacrifices. This bearer of mostly bad news has succeeded since its invention in transforming *homo sapiens* into *homo interruptus*.

It stands accused also of murdering the elegance of human communication. Writing letters, an activity of the hand that used to connect intelligence to affection and subtlety, has all but disappeared under its brutal buzz.

If I seem paranoid, consider the fact that the fate of the world hinges on a red telephone. And it occurs to me just now, that Edgar Allan Poe, who was prophetic and profoundly sad, had already garnered the true nature of the telephone long before it became a household word. Perched there by the bust of Pallas, it could be nothing else. The raven, with its "Nevermore!" is a telephone. The weird, omen-heavy bird of our poet of sorrow is a large, black telephone.

Wrong Number

I have never lived in a city where so many people call the wrong number. Ten times a day in New Orleans the phone rings and somebody asks for Florence or Mort or Spanky. "No Florence here," I say. That would stop people in most places. Not here. They go on talking to Florence as if I were just someone on the extension. I slam the phone down. Thirty seconds later it rings. Florence, Mort, or Spanky, please.

I told this to a native. He laughed. This city, he said, is famous for wrong numbers. I got an answering machine and said my name and number on it, and people leave messages for Florence, Mort, or Spanky. Or worse, they keep talking to them as if they were there. What I do now, see, is to say: "I'm so sorry. Florence had an accident. She's dying at Mercy Hospital. And Mort is dead. And Spanky's been hit by the streetcar."

Now I *could* do that. But it might not be enough. Another native told me that often the calls *are* for dead people. People call the old numbers, believing that the dead to whom that number once belonged will answer. There is a telephonic voodoo cult in the city. It's an old New Orleans practice, based on the belief that a person's phone number passes with the person's soul into the beyond. Something similar must have been on the minds of the people who buried Mary Baker Eddy, the founder of Christian Science. They put a phone in her grave waiting for her to call. On the other end, in a small office, a church official waits.

Good work, if you can get it.

But to return to the problem at hand: there *is* some evidence that the practice brings results. Either that, or people exasperated at being called Florence, Mort, or Spanky, finally admit that they are.

Call me Florence.

The New Body

A new, unsteady kind of creature lurches forth on the deserted streets of America these days. It is The Walking Driver. You can tell immediately that these beings are not true pedestrians: they waddle, they are unsteady, they have little back-of-the-head vision, they seem unused to the true weight of their bodies. They are not bipeds, nor are they four-legged creatures: they are semi-bipeds, sitting, folded creatures. A Martian observing the lunch hour in one of our cities said to me that an American without a car is gravely ill, like a snail that lost its shell. In fact, an American body is only a "body" when it is inside an automobile. What we see "walking" is only part of the body.

The American body, my friend explained, is an aggregation of man and machine. The latest addition to it is the computer. Very soon, a body not seated in front of a blinking screen can be considered as ill as a body outside of a car. My Martian friend, who has been a passionate observer of *Homo Americanus* since the nineteenth century, foresees a day when all newly born humans will have a plug inserted at the small of their back.

There is no doubt that the new symbiosis has occured: a new kind of criminal has already appeared. That's a sure proof because only criminals take reality seriously, thus legitimizing it. This is a new kind of thief, called an Indoor Hoodlum. His métier is to enter your computer with his computer to steal your thoughts. It is a different kind of crime, to be sure. A machine enters another machine. An old-fashioned criminal might well ask: Where is the thrill? Where is that shiver of pleasure and dread in a body engaged in surreptitious entry? Where is the physicality of the act? The sexuality of it? Delinquency has finally been taken off the streets and put where it belongs: in the home.

The Walking Driver is a highly artificial phenomenon. He walks for Health, or Well-Being, or other some such notion. He is walking Nowhere. When he means to go somewhere, he gets inside his car-body and sits before his computer-body.

In joining up with machines, my Martian friend notes, the machines do not become more human. You become more machinelike.

The Found Tribe

The latest news from the mimetic war front is that a new tribe is loose upon the land. They are the Wannabees. They are numerous as the leaves of grass, and there is no end to all the people they wanna be. They cluster together in groups at street corners giving the casual passerby a powerful jolt of recognition, followed by an equally powerful shock of quantity. Instead of one famous person, the passerby sees several of that person.

It all began with the cult of Madonna, the rock star not the virgin. Then there was Prince, who begat Princes and Princesses. When their tribes were sufficiently increased, there followed the Big Boom of Anybody Wannabees. There are now Rodney Dangerfield Wannabees and Joan Collins Wannabees. Most Wannabees originate from MTV, but some come from as far as the tabloids. In New Orleans they hang out at places called Déjà Vu. They thus sharply distinguish themselves from that Yuppie faction known as Willbees, who hang out at places called Que Sera.

After one gets over the shock of seeing so many Madonnas, let's say, one realizes that in one form or another the Wannabees have always been with us. In the fifties there were the Elvis Wannabees, in the sixties, the Beatles. At Mardi Gras there are boys who wanna be girls, so you can see lots of Marilyn Monroes and Tallulah Bankheads. It is possible that the Wannabees have existed in some form since the beginning of time: there have always been people who wanted to be someone else. It is possible also that we are all secretly Wannabees: everyone knows what a drag it is being oneself.

Whatever the history, however, the new Wannabees mean

business. A recent survey showed that most young Americans shown a map do not know where they live. Well, now it doesn't matter. It's not where you are but where you wanna be.

Nouveau Pirates

New Orleans is a pirate city, both in legend and fact. It is no wonder then that as soon as I disembarked—from the 4:20 Greyhound from Baton Rouge—I ran into privateers. What happened was that I walked into the first bar I saw to order a cold beer.

"Beer," I said, "It's hell out there."

It was only then that I looked at the bartender. A red scar traversed his face like a bolt of lightning from one corner of a marbleslab chin to a closed purple ostrich-egg of an eye.

"It's hell in here," he said.

Verily. Uncomfortably close to my left was a wrinkled midget with a scorpion face wearing a sleeveless T-shirt. His arms and shoulder were tattooed with layers of vicious symbols and proper names belonging to both sexes. He was muttering to himself something that sounded like: "I killed thirty-six people and I'm still hungry!"

On my right was an enormous cowboy with a huge hat and no shirt. Waves of flesh rolled away from him into the carved edge of the bar. One of his arms, the size of a regular person, was around a haggard wench with sagging everything, who sported also a number of wavy and faded tattoos that looked as if they'd been recently dug out in Pompei.

I took two gulps of beer, noting in passing that the glass hadn't been washed in anything but beer, and was quite possibly crawling with things you can only get in three or four places on earth.

I stepped over a few sprawled bodies on my way out the door, and marveled at my great fortune when I was actually on the other side of it. The merciless sun of New Orleans beat on my head like Jean Lafitte, the blacksmith pirate, beating a horseshoe in his forge.

When I got home, I walked into the serenity of my house and fondly watched my well-educated fourteen-year-old son work on his middle-class computer.

"How ya doing?" I said cheerily, trying to banish hell from my nostrils.

"I'm pirating a program," he said. "I get seasick, so I became a computer pirate instead."

He smiled that sweet fourteen-year-old smile, you know.

Cookin'

I've been passing by this store on my way to school, and it never fails to charm me. The hand-lettered sign in the window advertises new things every day: Gator, Coon, Possum, Garfish, Alligator. Any given day, at least three of those will be present.

Having only recently ventured to taste crawfish, I look forward to the rest of it.

Chef Paul Prudhomme may be making Cajun cooking pretty famous in the rest of the country, but people down here go by other lights. Justin Wilson's *Gourmet & Gourmand Cookbook* is a great authority. He has recipes for everything from alligator to venison, including the mighty strange Dishwasher Fish.

You wrap your fish in tinfoil and put it in your dishwasher with your dirty dishes. When they're clean, it's done.

There are literally hundreds of homemade cookbooks everywhere. They have things like Drunk Squirrel, Microwave-baked Juicy Swamp Rabbit, Opelousas's Baked Long Island Duck, Smothered Doves (Oh, Picasso! Oh, Paloma!), Garfish *en croute*, Frog Legs Congo Square, Gator Meatballs and Fried Alligator, Tipsy Turkey and Dove Pie, Blackbirds and Brown Rice, Bacon-baked Quail, Stuffed Teals—I have no idea what teals are (maybe the Audubon Society hotline can tell me)—and a huge potroast of dove, quail, snipe, squirrel, pheasant, or rabbit.

I don't know when I'll get around to all these things, but I won't go until I've had alligator sauce piquant. I hope it doesn't taste like the inside of a purse.

All these dishes come with explanations like "how to skin a deer in five minutes," and other handy hints.

Here is a quick recipe for Sally's Armadillo, from the *Cane*

River Cuisine Cookbook, put out by the Service League of
Natchitoches:

Clean the armadillo like a turtle. Marinate for 24 hours in
salad dressing. Pour a quart of wine over it and refrigerate for 6
hours. Brown sausage and armadillo in iron skillet. Serve over
rice. Use the shell for fortune-telling.

Guns

I took a pacifist, vegetarian friend of mine to this big sporting goods store down here. Add to my friend's credit the fact that he's from New York, and you have a perfect target to tease. The store in question is wallpapered with pistols. Even the ceiling is done in pistols. Everything from derringers to Civil War Colt revolvers festoon the place. They tell me that there used to be a rifle here until not so long ago with the caption, The Rifle That Killed Kennedy, but that may be apocryphal. In any case, there was plenty for my friend to get disgusted about. Here and there in the store stand the huge stuffed bodies of bears, deer, and foxes. And wherever there is room between pistols, they've got the innocent looking head of some creature peering at you. The guns on the walls are old. The guns in the glass cases are new. You can take your pick of anything from a pearl-handled revolver to an Uzi machine gun. A young office worker was in fact engaged in deep conversation with the salesman, trying to make just that kind of decision. "One of these would be nice," she said, cocking a Magnum pistol. She put it to her eye and took aim somewhere over the head of my New York friend. But he wasn't afraid.

"You know," he said, "until this Bernhard Goetz thing, everybody thought that New York wasn't part of America. Now I think they might be willing to let us back in."

Maybe. The back door was open and parked there was a huge, shiny-looking mobile home. Written on the side of it in huge black letters was: BIG MIKE'S BAIL BONDS. 24 HOURS. Now I'm not one to argue. Who's gonna run out on Big Mike? I could just see him, driving into city slums at night. Rejoyce, ye crooks, Big Mike's in town!

My friend said, "How about a soyburger?"

The office worker put down the Magnum. "Wrap it up," she said.

South

_____

No wonder great novelists come from the South. There is more room under the half-closed eyelids to observe the world at this pace. I'm not saying the South is slow, but I have certainly become slower since arriving here. I'm even thinking about sitting under that superb Spanish moss in my front yard, which also includes the Mississippi River, and writing a great novel called *Light in August*.

The whole country, or so it seemed from the interstate, is moving South. U-Hauls loaded with hope and mattresses streamed endlessly this way. As the vegetation grew wilder, the voices more honeyed, the churches more numerous, the food better, a kind of ancient giddiness possessed me. The proliferation of life that began somewhere in southern Virginia began to grow out of all reasonable proportion in Tennessee and Mississippi. It became an irresistible flood in Louisiana, where there were dead armadillos along the side of the road. Time itself underwent a subtle but decisive transformation. I felt tropical, fragrant, and observant.

I am of the school that maintains that migration is good for the soul. I believe with the Hopi Indians that one must cross the earth up and down and sideways before finding one's center. I have lived in the East, the West, and the North. The South is a personal necessity, even if it weren't for its ancient fascination. Since Cortes, everyone wanted to go South. Some, like Cortes's lieutenant Pisarro, went too far South. The jungle swallowed him, with the immoderation that all vegetal life seems to delight in here. But Pisarro was a soldier, not a novelist. Had he been a novelist, he would have written something like *One Hundred Years of Solitude*. Or should *I* write that?

Tales

———

They sho' like to tell tales down South. When we first got here, there was the question of getting some furniture. No problem, someone said, the whole town's full of yard sales. People here are so crazy about yard sales they come right into your house and try to buy your samplers right off the wall. Just the other day somebody offered to buy my old car *and* the lawn chairs.

Well, that's funny, I said, because just before I got here somebody from these parts told me that there was no furniture down here. In fact, all they had was one department store, and that was so crowded you could just never shop.

Next, the guy from the phone company came to turn on the phone. "You'll really enjoy it here," he said, "because it's summer all year around. It only gets cold one day before Christmas. But then," his voice took on an ominous hue here, "it gets *so* cold that people slide all over the place. We had twenty-two accidents on one block . . ." After he was done with the phone, he said: " 'Course, people are gonna tell you things about floodin'. Don't listen to 'em. It never floods. It flooded only once, about five years ago . . ." That hue again: "It was bad! Everything washed away, includin' downtown!"

I noticed too that people are always willing to help, no matter what. In fact, they have a passion for it. Ask someone for directions. No problem. Elaborate, kind directions follow, spiced here and there with a little background on people who lived on this or that street on the way to where you're going. Only trouble is, after circling the area several times, you're nowhere near the place.

This place may well be the salvation of literature. They still know the value of a good yarn down here.

Two Men and a Boy

I tiptoe around religion and ritual. I would rather be swimming in subfreezing weather than be caught in a theological dispute. And yet, there is no ignoring that little voice somewhere in the depths of the heart that says: "You can't deny evil so how about that other stuff?"

I normally pay no attention because I was raised a strict atheist. In my Communist school I was told that "religion was the opiate of the people" and from my own observation I could tell that only old people went to church. They moved slowly and they hid their faces, which made me think that old age itself was an opiate. After all, young people, the way they showed us on posters, moved energetically forward in the name of Progress. But I wasn't convinced.

Perhaps if it had been only the going to church my doubts may have subsided. But I was also a Jew, a fact I didn't understand very well. I was clearly different and my difference had something to do with religion. I tried not to think about it.

The other day I went to a synagogue for the first time in my life. After the service, three of us took a slow walk up the cobblestones of an old street, talking. Two of us were about the same age, though raised differently. The other was a ten-year-old boy.

"I would give my left eyeball to know why I participate in a meaningless ritual that doesn't do much for me," said my friend and sucked furiously on his pipe.

I would have done anything to save his eye, but I knew that no explanation would have satisfied him. He was asking that question precisely because the ritual had meant something. Otherwise, he wouldn't have been so violently metaphorical.

"It is the power of the words themselves as they are written down and spoken," I tried to explain.

I told him how once, when I had been the age of the young boy walking with us, I'd been taken by a friend of mine to the ruin of an ancient synagogue in my medieval hometown. The place was overgrown with weeds and had fallen into disuse because all the Jews in town, with a few assimilated exceptions like myself, had gone to Israel. I remember seeing Hebrew letters for the first time in that dark place. They glowed and shimmered with a life entirely their own. Later we went into a barn where we saw the old synagogue hearse, black, with those mysterious letters written in gold on the side of it. They were really glowing. I experienced a profound awe and amazement, not free of terror, as I stood before something I had never known. I can't describe that feeling now, too many years have passed. But it was decidedly disproportionate to the objects in question.

"Well, yes," my friend admitted, "I did feel an odd familiarity, a comfort and a sense of mystery. What are you thinking about?" he asked the boy.

"About a cartoon. This man was having trouble with his engine so he took it out and put it in the back seat of the car. When he took the key out of the ignition he turned it just once to see if it still turned and the motor started working in the back seat. All the fan blades and everything were going and the car started moving *up* like a helicopter."

The boy was not usually given to *non sequitur* so the two gentlemen paid close attention to his contribution. A cartoon certainly, but at another level the boy illustrated perfectly the matter at hand. Religion, of all things, exists precisely because it defies the definitions and reasons for which men lose their eyeballs. If it is possible for an engine to start in the back seat, it is possible for God to take root in the heart of a rationalist. Miracles are, after all, the shortest explanation.

The two gentlemen and the boy then stopped at a café for two cognacs and a cherry Coke. They raised their glasses and toasted each other's health. They played a game of pool. It was definitely a holiday.

"It is astounding how hard it is to admit the existence of these religious feelings," said the furious pipe smoker, putting the cue ball in instead of the six. "It's as if they were a bigger secret than sex."

"Indeed they are," I said.

"During the last part of the service I started singing 'We all live in a yellow submarine,'" said the boy.

The men had to doff their hats to him. (They weren't wearing any, so they bowed their heads.) The boy wasn't afraid of having those feelings or of being irreverent. Yes, it is definitely better to be ten.

After the game they strolled past an old wharf where, behind tall black-eyed Susans, several fishermen sat smoking.

"Got anything?" I asked.

"Look for yourself," the old man said.

We all looked. In the bucket next to him were about twenty respectable fish.

"A year ago a guy comes here and tells me there ain't no fish because of pollution," laughs the old man.

On the way back, the boy gathers a few black-eyed Susans for his mother. "One-eyed Susans," he said.

The sky is blue. An October breeze blows. In this light, all is resolved.

Oh Dad, Poor Dad

At times I consider myself fortunate to have grown up without a father to beat me over the head. I roamed the streets and did delicious and forbidden things which would have certainly aroused the ire of a father, even a mild one.

But at other times, I feel the regret too of having never known him. What did he think? Who was he? I made up all sorts of stories about him when I was a kid. He became by turns a hero, an artist, a fighter. The real man? Who knows?

In Western culture, father always has a stick in his hand. Until Freud revealed him as the villain of the family drama, the father had a pretty unassailable position in the value system of Judaeo-Christian civilization. In Judaism, God the Father is stern, unforgiving, vengeful, and just. He is prone to fits of anger, great displays of rage and, equally, incomprehensible bouts of affection. His emotions come big and he cannot stand the questioning of his authority.

Most earthly fathers in our world modeled themselves after the heavenly one. Jesus tried to reform the crusty old geezer by insisting that God the Father was a god of forgiveness and love as well. In my opinion, he succeeded only in making a few rare souls think about it. In reality, God didn't give an inch of his image.

In older cultures, the magic ones of Oceania and Egypt, the responsibility for the world did not devolve entirely upon the shoulders of the father. The earthly fathers must have been breathing easier when the matriarchal deities of moon, earth, tides, and seasons governed the world. Those feminine deities followed the circular motions of nature and were the figurative opposites of the pyramidal hierarchy of authority, civilization, and war. The fathers of those days must have been kindly creatures.

As descendants of the patriarchal Greeks, Jews, and Romans, we know little of that old religion. In our culture, the paternal interest of the state in the behavior of its citizens has always encouraged real fathers to be as severe as possible. The state reasons that well-disciplined children make well-disciplined soldiers. Until World War I, in fact, few people thought there was anything wrong with the vision of God the Father, the Paternal State and the Head of the Family.

There were, of course, dissensions, remnants perhaps of an ancient past or signs of a spontaneous equilibrium. The love cults of the Middle Ages (notably the Albigensians, the Troubadours, and the Bogomilians) questioned paternal authority on behalf of emotions and reasons of the heart. Naturally, both the church and the state burned all those disbelievers at the stake. Heresy in the Western world, until the eighteenth century, meant only one thing: messing with the father image.

The real fathers were, I believe, the losers of these symbolic wars. But in order to know them, we had to unravel them. Beginning with Freud, we have been doing a fine job of it. We have unfairly saddled them with reason, calling it their form of thinking. Our emotional life, our "secret" history, our longings, we have relegated to the feminine half.

Being a Viennese and a Victorian, Freud put all this very nicely into the black-and-white language of science. But others, like Franz Kafka, didn't need that excuse. His father's words of admonition, he says, have "traced positive furrows in my brain."

After the Second World War, faith in almost everything was shattered. The first philosophical movement to poke its weary head from the ruins of Europe was existentialism, which found nothing worth fighting for any longer. The contemporary "revolt against the fathers" began there and continues unabated today. It wasn't a matter solely for philosophers. In the late 1950s and the 1960s, youth became a "culture," rejecting the values of the fathers.

The women's liberation movement drove stakes right through the heart of remaining paternal myths. Supported by statistics which show an increasing number of women raising their children without fathers, the revolt grows.

And yet. Poor fathers. Where are they? Seeping through the cracks in the sidewalks of vast, inhuman cities? Working their lives away in factories, chained to assembly lines? And those who do raise their children, what connection do they still have to the shape of our world? Can we honestly say that their authority reflects that of the multinational corporations? Hardly. If anything, the powers that get away with our lives are genderless, neuter, and probably faceless.

Now that I am a father myself, I try to make myself known without using that accursed stick too much or, at least, by taking it easy with my paternal tradition. The burden of it is there, though, no question about it.

A Father-Son Talk with the Animals

Four fat turkeys spread their plumes and trumpeted in unison
their displeasure at something I could not see. Their trembling
fleshly necklaces and those nose ornaments that look like exterior
tongues turned red, purple, and magenta.

I said: "Are you mad at the world situation? Are you tired of
being eaten?" But even as I said it, I knew that that wasn't it.
Something else, news of another order, had come down the bird
telegraph, and they were expressing their opinion.

I next visited the snowy owl and looked into its yellow eyes,
cracked by a black exclamation point in the middle. The owl's
eyes were mammal eyes, the eyes of a cat. It leaped away from
me on two furry legs, the legs of Conan the Barbarian. "Tell me,
owl," I said, "How many months before I cross the ocean?" The
owl looked up in the sky, and nodded. Up there, a flock of
crows cawed four times. "Four months then?" The wise bird
nodded again.

At the golden eagle's roost, my four-year-old son asked: "Do
you open your wings wide when you fly or do you keep them
closed, eagle?" The golden eagle, high above our petty intentions and questions, looked for a moment as if he hadn't heard
him. But then a claw came up and he scratched his curved, hard
beak. He then opened his wings suddenly, for their whole
magnificent span, and flew a short distance. "Thank the eagle," I
said. "Thank you eagle!" said son.

A ways down the winding road, a father antelope with long,
sharp horns was teaching his son how to fight. The son, down
on his knees in the mud, tried desperately to hook his horn
under his father's head. But try as he might, he always met only
the harder and bigger horns of his father. Watching with

considerable apprehension, two other members of the family paced in the mud.

The American buffalo, once numbering two million, and now numbering a mere ten thousand, looked on us sullenly like a head on a nickel. He reminded me less of himself than of a Jimez pueblo shaman with a buffalo headdress. I expected him to stand on two legs and dance.

Afterward, we went to a little medieval village in Holland, except the village was a pond and the villagers were ducks. The villager ducks were having some sort of feast. They splashed, rolled over, made windmills out of their wings, craned their necks, screamed. The bigger ducks splashed the little ducks and the little ducks splashed them back. A proud, lone black and white duck preened delicately away from the crowd.

Not far from there, the flamingos had turned bright pink since we had last seen them. Pink, which is a sign of old age in flamingos, flared brilliantly over a few remaining black and brown feathers. Lined up like question marks in orderly rows, they seemed to be asking existential clarification from the cold, pale blue sky. "Why age? Why so soon?" Having the same kind of inquiry in my own heart, I nodded gravely. "When you find out," I said, "let me know." The flamingos have time to look at the sky for answers. I must type.

We move on. My son said that he must find the parrot. On our way there, we passed the earth's strangest creatures, the ostriches. The pathetic little fluff of undistinguished hair atop their tiny heads was ruffled by the cold wind. Solidly planted in the muddy earth, their long, sad feet seemed bound there by a huge, cosmic joke. The vast bodies with the feather-duster feathers stood atop those comedy sticks like props in a silent movie. There is something so touching about you, I wanted to say. Something that reminds me of myself. But I didn't say it because I knew that the ostriches wouldn't hear me. Unlike the very intelligent birds we had just visited, the ostrich has only its sad shape for a thought. It hears nothing, it is always confused.

The parrot was waiting for us. "I am cold!" he shrieked. "Take me back to Matto Grosso!" "Yeah!" the toucan next door joined in: "Back to Bolivia!" And the kookaburra screamed above the din: "Kukaburra sits . . . in the old gum tree . . . no more . . . eating all the gumdrops . . . he can't see . . . stop kukaburra . . . stop."

And it was cold. But not cold enough for the brown bears to sleep. One was turning over, and the other hugged a log. "Happy to see you," one of them said. "I miss the summer crowd."

At the leopard's cage, I looked into the impassive eyes of the cat. We locked gazes. "Tyger, Tyger, burning bright . . . ," I said. Being called a tiger didn't upset him. He merely stared past me at something dim and quick in his animal memory.

It was a wintry day, sunny and cold. We were the animals' only visitors at the Baltimore Zoo. Spring was far off. At the gate I remembered Whitman:

I think I could turn and live with animals, they're so placid and self-contain'd,
I stand and look at them long and long.

Getting Drug-Wise

"Hey," my son said, "they showed us more movies about heroin and LSD in school today!" He rolled down the car window.

"Great," I said. Every day for the past three weeks, they've been showing the kids drug movies in school. They started them out on aspirin. They were now graduating to harder drugs.

"Well, don't you want to know about LSD?" he insisted.

"What about LSD?" I took a large swig of lukewarm coffee.

"There are two kinds," he said. "Psycho something, on sugar cubes, and antihistamines . . ."

"Great word," I said. "Did they show you how after you take it your eyeballs roll in your head and you go like this . . . ?" I made an ugly face and roared like a wounded leprechaun or a thirsty zebra.

"No, but they had this kid being served a bowl of all kinds of pills, blue, green, and orange . . . and then they showed him going on to marijuana and then he goes downtown and takes heroin and then they put him in jail."

"He was lucky," I said. "He could've ended up dead. Or he could've ended up spending the night in the Trailways station. You never know with downtown."

You also never know who's on what.

I went downtown just the other day. A slightly disheveled businessman with a slightly open briefcase stopped me on Charles Street.

"Can you lend me a dollar?" he asked.

I'd never given anyone using that line more than a quarter. But here was this man, well dressed, with a briefcase. Didn't look like a bum. A great misfortune must have overtaken him. A green, blue, orange, or red pill mistakenly swallowed by the water cooler in his office. Then a little heroin. Blam! Before he knew it he was broke and begging. I gave him a dollar.

I told my son the story. "Drugs," I concluded.

But if the truth be known (I didn't want to overwhelm his young mind with too much of it at once), I'd been made a fool of. It would be easy to blame drugs. In reality, I'd been taken in by a suit. A wino or a junkie would have never gotten more than that quarter out of me. But a man in a suit!

"They showed us a glue movie too," said the son, ignoring both my story and my qualms.

"With model airplanes and all?"

"No. They found this kid dead with a glue bottle in his nose!"

"Why don't they just show you a pile of dead bodies laid out to spell D-R-U-G-S?" asked his mother, who was driving a barely functional Japanese car on a roaring American highway.

I took another large swig of bitter brew.

"I get a stomachache every time I look at those movies," my son confided.

"Don't take aspirin," I advised. "But I think the real reason you get a stomachache is because they are scaring you. You're going to be a generation of saints. I only saw *Reefer Madness* once, and I laughed until I cried. But when it came out, not everyone did. They outlawed marijuana right away, even though no one'd heard of it . . . ?"

"Marijuana," he said matter-of-factly, "that's what the kid with the pills went to next after he was through with the pills . . ."

"Wait. I thought it was antihistamines . . ."

"Dad!" he exclaimed impatiently, "Those are a kind of delusions . . ."

"I thought they were a kind of LSD . . ."

He furrowed his brow. "What's the use of telling you? You just don't know."

"Can't they teach you something nice? Like sex education?" asked his mother, my wife.

"Yeah, like how the stork drops a clean baby through the exhaust pipe of the mobile home? Or how large outer-space eggs get blown up by comets in the blue yonder? You should watch that movie." That's the kind of father I am. Give me a subject, no matter how educational, and I'll explain it in detail.

"I know all about sex," he said. "You get diseases."

"Diseases? Now who in the world told you that?"

"In school," he said. "Or somebody else. I don't remember."

"Some school. They dish you LSD and heroin together, they throw sex and diseases in the same bag, and they probably make you memorize it all for next day. Since when do sex and diseases get casually mentioned in the same breath?" I was getting worked up now. Here is a sweet mystery of the Creation itself, and they are putting diseases in the kids' heads. I'm not against sex education, but if they're going to drag out old Navy movies from decommissioned ships to show in classrooms, forget it.

"Let me tell you about school, son," I said. "Take everything with a couple of grains of salt . . ."

"Salt!" he exhaled, "It's bad for you."

"Not as bad as some of that . . ."

"Cut it out," mother and wife said. "You'll spill your coffee. And your stomachache will get worse!" She pressed down on the gas and a great plume of exhaust rose from behind us and joined with similar plumes at the intersection.

The sky was a metallic purple. We kept quiet.

Elena

———

Elena spared us. There are rains and wind now, but the brunt of it was to the northeast of us. For a few days there we lived through preparations reminiscent of war. Parts of New Orleans looked like a city preparing for a bombing raid: taped windows, boarded storefronts. A hurricane is in fact a bomb, a bomb filled with evil winds.

At the supermarket last night there were lines going all the way from the cash registers to the frozen food. Behind me was a girl from El Salvador who was having a good time, as was everybody else. This is just like home, she said. Yeah, I said, it is for me too. The lines reminded me of Romania in my child-hood, the only difference being that in Romania there was no food. Only lines.

This being New Orleans there were, of course, hurricane parties everywhere. Our neighborhood laundromat stayed open all night and advertised a hurricane party. The drink Hurricane is, as you may know, a local invention.

As the news that all the low-lying areas near the coast were being evacuated started to come in, I began to feel some apprehension. Everyone I talked to had a hurricane story. My friend Chuck said that the most vivid memory of his childhood was being woken in the middle of the night, bundled up, and put in the car. He remembers seeing the eye of the storm above him. That was Camille, and the locals still lower their voices when they mention her name.

There was no question of sleeping last night, so we stayed awake listening to civil defense engineers talking about the levees, police and army officials talking about large rescue projects. Incidentally, the radio is the medium of crisis, par excellence. It is much more intimate and trustworthy than television.

Elena didn't come—but I got a sense of living in the subtropics, a kind of initiation.

Technocracy's Spoor

A covert operation has been described as "having the fingerprints of the Russians all over it." The fingerprints of the CIA, of Castro, of Kaddafi have been found on so many things (boats, airplanes, bodies) that the image coming most readily to mind is one of huge hands, moving in the night, leaving the impressions of enormous thumbs and index fingers forever imprinted on the skulls and skins of the world's gullible folk.

The time has come to consider fingerprints seriously—*sub speciae eternitatis*—particularly in view of the fact that the astronauts on the first shuttle flight found the earth to be a grey, dirty mass of smudged fingerprints. The fingerprints, they could have added, of Dow Jones, Allied Chemical, Soviet industry, and Big Oil. The earth looks bad, they said, and it is getting worse: The filth is becoming homogenous. Soon we won't be able to tell whose fingerprints are where: The whole will be the single print of a choking hand. Gasp, gasp.

When we say that the president "has his finger on the button," we don't usually think of the fingerprint. But it's there, on the button. The same goes for the Soviet premier. His fingerprint is on the button, too. One can imagine two detective cockroaches, with luminous green skins, on the button, too. "This one is definitely the American's fingerprint, Watson." "Amazing, Sherlock, how did you do that?"

Fantomas, a very famous French criminal of the 1920s, was reputed to have made himself gloves from the skin of a dead man's hands in order to leave the wrong fingerprints behind.

Today, Fantomas would have been caught. A new method can "smoke" fingerprints right through thin rubber and plastic gloves. It can even lift prints from skin, plants, plastic bags, foam cups, and even hair. This product will soon be mass-manufactured and we will all become detectives. Holding bottles of fingerprint-lifting glue, jealous husbands will lift prints from their sleeping wives' hair. Suspicious employers will stay late to lift prints from the knobs of safes. Half of our time will be spent kneeling by telephones and doors with print-glue in our hands.

Of course, this stuff is only for little fingerprints. The fingerprints of countries, secret armies, and multi-national companies are too big to be lifted like that. Most likely, it will be they who will be lifting our fingerprints off everything, in order to ascertain whether we have been meddling in their affairs.

What exactly is a fingerprint? It is, foremost, a sign of our uniqueness. No two peoples' fingerprints are alike. This is a truly miraculous and stubborn fact in a world where we are daily encouraged to become similar. We are encouraged, for instance, to think that All Russians Are Bad, and therefore similar, and that Americans Should Buy What Is Advertised, which makes us similar as well. These two similar masses are then encouraged to pit their badness and their goodness against each other. The fingerprints of something horrible are all over this scheme, but of what, pray tell?

Whatever the thing is, uniqueness bothers it. The obnoxious individuality of every breathing thing, the glorious diversity of life bothers it. The fingerprint, in its ubiquitous visibility, stands arrogantly reminding each and every one of their irreducible humanity. We are single, unique, irreplaceable, unsubstitutable beings, say our fingerprints. You cannot assume that we will do, say, and think the same thing under any circumstances.

Actually, it is quite simple. Whatever it is that wants us to be the same would like our hands to be where they could be seen. Your fingers in the future should not be where they have no business being. They should be where they belong: on the keyboards during working hours, on the controls of electronic entertainment during leisure time.

Blip for the Hero

Time Magazine's Man-of-the-Year is a machine! At last! The computer chosen for the honor is a handsome thing. Wide-screened, slick, colorful, it is hundreds of times better at math than the paunchy humans previously enshrined.

There could be a number of reasons for the editors' decision. A quiet coup may have taken place at *Time,* and all the humans working there may have been stealthily replaced by the computers in the office. Next year's Man-of-the-Year will be a radar dish. The year after that, a curvaceous missile. An insignificant number will worry. They will dwindle away. By the end of the century, the machines will have enough confidence to feature a human on the cover of *Time,* as Man-of-the-Year.

Of course, by 1999 it will be hardly necessary to bother with humans. They will have become such malleable toys, the machines will be buying them for Christmas for junior computers to play with.

Even as long ago as World War I, a character in Stefan Zweig's novel *Beware of Pity* could say: "It is sheer nonsense nowadays to take into account the willingness or unwillingness of human material, for in the next war the actual fighting would be done by machines, and men would be reduced to no more than a kind of component part of the machine."

Further back even, there is the character of Thomas Edison in Villiers de l'Isle Adam's nineteenth-century fantasy, *Tomorrow's Eve,* building an android endowed with intelligence who takes over everyone's mind. A survey of fantasy and science-fiction books reveals a uniformly depressing vision. In most, if not all, the human world ends. There is some disagreement as to the nature of this end: some writers appear to prefer slow ecological poisoning to a bright, spectacular flash. But in all of them, machines do the actual "dirty work." Humans are left to do the dying.

A weak countermovement (spurred on by the machines themselves) is evident in sympathetic robots like R2D2, for instance, or in the melted-plastic friendliness of ET. But the sentimental machines are in trouble in all these stories: they have either been left behind, or are outdated, or they experience an imminent threat of termination. It is not the machines we feel sympathy for when this happens, but for ourselves, similarly being left behind, superseded, or terminated.

Of course, *Time* thinks it's for the best. But I wouldn't bet on it. I sleep in my clothes.

Missile Command

A trillion cosmic pings later, our nostalgia for the stars isn't what it used to be. I remember coming out of the premiere showing of *Close Encounters of the Third Kind* and looking at the night sky with something akin to sorrow, and thinking, "That is where we come from." A second later, I corrected myself: "This movie will do wonders for NASA." But I did not suspect, and few people did, that *Close Encounters,* like its predecessor *Star Wars,* would flood the earth with computer music, electronic aliens, eerie clicks, and hypnotic lights.

I saw the movie on television again the other day, and I was astounded to see how trite and bare it had become. I realized also how bad it was and how flawlessly the machinery of public taste is exploited. What impressed me in those bygone days of the premiere was the revelation of the yearning we all feel for the stars. It articulated an almost mystical desire to escape from the backwaters of the planet. Escape from the mess is the greatest human urge, and the movie made it seem possible when it made the stars big and beautiful, the alien lights resplendent, and the aliens wise and friendly. There is hope, the picture said.

There was hope, of course, for the budding video game industry that understood from it only that people will go for the form over the substance any day. The hope and nostalgia that provided for the success of the machinery were discarded like so much other "human" junk, and the pure clickety-clackety of computers took over.

On second viewing, *Close Encounters* looked, in fact, down-right inhuman. Why should we suppose that alien culture, should it exist, would make use of the same kind of plastic and neon technology that makes us sterile here on earth? Why not suppose, for instance, that if the aliens are truly intelligent they might prefer to develop along organic, cellular lines? Wouldn't they prefer living tissue over hardware?

The aliens in *The Invasion of the Body Snatchers* did prefer the living and growing over the dead and the metallic, but they were, unfortunately, hostile. They came to earth in the form of seed pods and made all the red-blooded Americans around them into soulless happy people. The unmistakable metaphor there was that the aliens were Communists and they were up to no good. Because of it, the movie, terrifying as it was, failed to create a craze either for seed pods or Communists.

Not until *Close Encounters* did anyone dare to treat the aliens well. The proviso, of course, was that the aliens be just like us, only in possession of better machines. The aliens, shown briefly at the end of the movie, are truly ugly, and I don't think anybody can tolerate them for longer than a few seconds. The implication is that humans may be just as disgusting to them, but what does all that matter when we have something so much better in common, namely, those blinking puddles of circuits and clicking switches? The inevitable conclusion is that humans are obsolete, that machines know better. No wonder a whole enthusiastic industry was born from that premise. To the people in charge of our lives these days, humans are a nuisance.

I saw another film, a few years ago, pointing in a slightly different direction. It was called *The Man Who Fell to Earth,* and in it, the alien landed on this planet by accident and was able to get by just fine, thanks to his advanced knowledge and the American way. In that movie, removable eyeballs didn't stand in the way of true love. On the contrary, they added to it. Alien eccentricities were forgiven him since he was a rich man. For all that he was royally bored among all the well-meaning and scheming earthlings and would have done anything to go back home. The novelty of seeing the alien as an individual and even identifying with him was utterly bracing. I remember looking at the night sky after seeing that movie, too, and thinking: "One day, I'm coming home." It had been revealed to me that I was more of an alien than my regular terrestrian habits might suggest.

In a sense, I think that our society stands at the crossroads suggested by these three versions of the future: Engage the planet in a technological race that assigns humans only the positions of their efficiency, revive the ideological cold war through nationalistic fervor (i.e., We are better than Them), and, finally, look for the human in us. The human in us is the true alien today. We are stranger to ourselves than we can imagine.

Does a Proton Laugh?

To all those who doubt that the future, in its most futuristic form, is already here, I offer the following domestic scene: I am reading *Grunch of Giants,* Buckminster Fuller's last book; through the closed doors come the space pings of my son's relentless struggle against Space Invaders; lying open on my desk is President Reagan's latest pitch for Star Wars.

GRUNCH is an acronym for "Gross Universal Cash Heist," and it is Bucky's name for the monstrous agglomeration of multinational corporations that gets away with what should be commonly held wealth. Bucky was not a Marxist. Right at the beginning, he states: "The author is apolitical. I was convinced in 1927 that humanity's most fundamental survival problems could never be solved by politics."

In 1927, Bucky set out to help the world: His beginnings coincide with technological integration of the planet. In 1927, a human first flew alone across the ocean in one day. And Bucky began inventing: the Dymaxion House, the one-piece 250-pound bathroom, Synergetics, the Dymaxion World Map, Geodesic Domes, twin-hull rowing and sailing devices, and on and on. It is like reading a fairy tale: The world changes at ever-increasing speed, from isolated countries to Spaceship Earth. But now suddenly we are at a great dangerous crossroads: Either we change our way of thinking or we will be "terminated."

In the other room, there is no end of Space Invaders. They come down in disciplined, relentless rows, shooting lasers at the tattered shield of the sole defender. As their numbers are thinned, they panic. They begin moving at ever-increasing speeds in a desperate effort to land. But the defender is sharp: He shoots down the last of them with a satisfying plop. But no sooner is the first expedition checked, a second board full of invaders appears. These new ones are meaner, faster and closer to the ground. The sacrifice of the first crew has not been in vain: certain information has survived. The defender in the next room is good: He destroys seven ships before he is destroyed by the eighth. The sad fizzling sound of the exhausted hero fills the house with sorrow. It's not who wins but how you play the game, echoes the mournful wisdom of humanity. But not to worry: Push a switch and you can start again.

Not so, says Bucky: If we blow this one there is no second chance. "The failure of humans means the function must be performed in local-Universe by other phenomena capable of reliably serving the information-agglomerating and problem-solving function. The eternal Universe show must go on." Bucky is an optimist: First, he sees earthlings achieving a possible Golden Age through technology. Then, if that doesn't work, he sees the Universe—minus the humans—Golden Aging all on its own.

I am not so generous. I think of these "other phenomena" that would replace us and I get the creeps. What could they be? Electromagnetic waves? Pulses? Electrons? Does a proton laugh? Can a volt weep? I don't want to be replaced by any of them, thank you. Call it old neo-platonic stubbornness.

And then there is the president's cosmic war budget. The weapons he is proposing resemble those of my son's, only they are bigger. He wants the children to like and understand these things. GRUNCH is nice, he likes to play . . .

Bucky again: "We can very properly call WW I the million-dollar war and WW II the billion-dollar war and WW III the trillion-dollar war. The number of dollars the USA and the USSR have already spent on armaments since the end of WW II, since the United Nations was established, is 6 trillion."

That is roughly what the US program alone is going to cost in the next ten years. Six trillion dollars!

"Six and one-half trillion is the number of miles radiation reaches out radially in one year, traveling at 186,000 miles per second. That is the magnitude of the number of dollars the supranational corporations are now intent on spending, and spending exclusively on killingry, at the same time that old people are deprived of their security and children go lunchless." Go, Bucky!

No wonder GRUNCH would like to make friends with the kids. They believe in fairy tales. "It becomes very plausible that our observed universe emerged from nothing or almost nothing," says Dr. Alan Guth of MIT.

OK, but do we have to go back to nothing?

Links

It started with the clock. I remember when I put the clock on top of the radio. The time was 1976. Next time I looked, the clock was inside the radio. They had merged. The time was 1979. I put the clock-radio next to the phone. Next time the phone rang it was from inside the clock-radio. I picked up the receiver and talked as I listened to the news and noted the time. It was 1981. During my absence from the house one time, I came back to find the telephone-answering machine inside the clock-radio-phone. The weird mating accelerated in the months that followed. The telephone-answering-clock-radio-phone married the tapedeck. The telephone-answering-clock-radio-phone-tapedeck married the turntable and the speakers. The telephone-answering-clock-radio-phone-tapedeck-turntable-speakers married the TV. The telephone-answering-clock-radio-phone-tapedeck-turntable-speakers-TV married the home computer. The telephone-answering-clock-radio-phone-tapedeck-turntable-speakers-TV-computer married the modem. The year was 1984. The telephone-answering-clock-radio-phone-tapedeck-turntable-speakers-TV-computer-modem married the modem in the house next door. The two modems—which were each part of a telephone-answering-clock-radio-phone-tapedeck-turntable-speakers-TV-computer system—began to marry other modems up and down the street. These group marriages accelerated rapidly. I looked at the clock, its faint pulse barely visible in the large body around it. The time was 1984. Breathing evenly around me was the telephone-answering-clock-radio-phone-tapedeck-turntable-speakers-TV-computer-modem-bank-store-moviehouse-restaurant. When I was finished observing the rapidly growing electronic mass, I felt the sharp prodding of something metalic in my back as a jack slipped neatly into a socket at the base of my spine. I then typed this on my keyboard which is also the table where I work and take my meals. The time is 1985. I don't have to look at the clock to tell you.

The Disillusioned

Dear Computer,

This is a Dear John letter. It's all over between us. I'm going back to the old fountain pen, if I can still find one. I remember how proud I used to be in my youth that, as a poet, all I needed was a pencil stub and a paper bag. Failing that, a razor blade and a wall.

Here I am now, in my dotage, standing in five and one quarter inches of disk plastic trying to be *deep*. Don't make me laugh. Everyone I talk with these days tells me how disappointed they are in you: they thought you could make them faster, slicker, richer. You only made them longwinded, blinder, and cheaper. Longwinded because they've all been writing more than they meant to, blinder because your screen is venomous, and cheaper because the demand for their work has gone down as the copies multiplied.

I heard that the warplanes of the future aren't going to have any windows. Instead, the pilot will see a computer-generated picture of the landscape he is flying over. This picture is not the *actual* landscape but a structural composite rebuilt by you. In other words, he will be watching a movie you have told him is real. But, you know, killing just won't be the same without windows. What is it about you that causes you to always abstract and abstract? Couldn't you enhance instead? Instead of a few sketchy lines, you could give the pilot the details of the faces he is about to blast into oblivion. That would be the poetic thing to do.

But no, doing that would go against your nature, which is to abstract and abstract until no particulars intrude. Another of my friends, who has recently fallen to your apparent charm, in spite of my warnings, told me that she gave you a nice, human name. That, I think, was a mistake. In a few months, at the very latest, you will begin to steal her soul. It may already be too late to leave you. I wonder, even as I type, if I am not already like one of those pilots in his windowless planes. I may be doing your work even as I say my goodbye. In fact, I may have just written your goodbye to me, thinking it my own.

The Keyboards of Silence

The Romanian government just banned typewriters. Persons
with a record and especially persons under suspicion of dis-
tributing unauthorized literary material cannot now own one of
these things I am furiously pounding. This strange bit of news
comes to me at an ironic juncture: I am shopping for a word
processor.

As a measure of the distance I have traveled, this coincidence
has no peer. The geographical miles are insignificant compared
to the psychic miles between a place that is trying to ban
typewriters and a place that is having a price war on computers.

I remember the emotion I felt at sixteen, in my Romanian
home town, when I first sat down at a typewriter. The machine
belonged to an older friend of mine, a writer who also did
mysterious things for the police. Before he let me use it, to copy
my handwritten poems, he warned me that the serial numbers of
all the typewriters in the country were on file with the police.
He then dramatically uncovered the statuesque, black body of an
old Underwood, and left me alone with it.

I flexed my fingers. I caressed the keys slightly. It was an
important moment: my poems were about to make the passage
from the dreamy intimacy of handwriting to the metallic responsibility of public domain. This passage presaged awesome
things, of which I was only vaguely aware. In some way, this
imminent transformation of my work reflected my own, from a
boy to a man. I was fully awake to the awesome ritualistic
import of the act I was about to perform.

My friend's warning put a further edge of excitement on the
operation: not only was I allowed to use the grownups' public

voice, but I was also capable of dissenting now, of saying something that my handwriting had been incapable of.

I looked at my poor handwritten works, looking already much too feeble for the transformation awaiting them. They seemed to glow with a far-off nostalgic light, as if they belonged to my receding childhood. When my friend came home, he found me with my handwritten poems strewn on the floor all around me. The typewriter lay untouched. The initiation had to take place some other time.

It wasn't until I left Romania that I could sit at a typewriter and just type, as if it were a normal thing to do. By then, things had changed. I didn't care for handwriting anymore. I liked the staccato din of modern American life. I liked the typewriterlike hum of New York and its rushing humans, who looked to me like the madly dancing keys of a shiny, vast keyboard. America moved at the speed of its keyboards, and I wasn't about to dwell in the past. I began composing directly on the typewriter, as I am doing now.

When I finish a novel or a book of poetry I save the ribbon. Last time I went to Europe, I lugged my typewriter with me, a real pain it was, too, dragging the metal beast through airports and hotels. But I didn't want to leave this matter to chance: Europe, at least the Europe I remembered, was the place of silence, sadness, registered serial numbers, and handwriting.

In school, when I was growing up, they told us about the weapons of the Revolution: the typewriter and the mimeograph machine. These early technological wonders of our century were deemed more dangerous than guns and bombs. In the sad, medieval dictatorship of Romania, that hackneyed notion still holds. A single high-speed IBM copier could unsettle the whole house of cards.

I've already pretty much decided what word processor to get. But now I am not so sure. Perhaps I should look back for a while, and wait. Perhaps I should write by hand and remember.

Symbols

I am looking at a news photo that contains in its stark contradictions one of the great images of our time, and I am filled with wonder. Here is the story of our time: the Holy Virgin of the Polish strike on the Gdansk shipyard gate and the statue of Lenin!

The remarkable thing is not their seeming proximity but their interaction. What is remarkable is the light that the Virgin throws on Lenin. The citizens of Eastern Europe and the Soviet Union are used to the ubiquitous statuary of Communism. They go about their business without a glance at the race of marble and bronze giants watching them from above. This is as it should be: no one can live with the dread of knowing that they are permanently dwarfed by the Idea Fathers.

The Lenin of Gdansk had been gathering dust for years until the arrival of the Virgin of the Strike. Suddenly, the unnoticing eyes of the people are on him. A new scrutiny, a new look, a profound, startled gaze. The uncomfortable possibility of being pulled out by the roots.

I remember the feeling of utter relief, upon leaving Romania, at having gotten away from the oversized portraits and statues of the eternal scrutinizers of the Party, and seeing over my head, not Lenin's cap, Stalin's boot, or Ceausescu's triple chin, but gorgeous women holding chocolates and shampoos. The scale of the images was the same but their effect was most decidedly not. Where the Fathers of Communism castigated, invoked guilt, and punished, the advertisements enticed, cajoled, and seduced. I have since grown wary of the underlying themes of most advertising, but still . . . would you rather be scolded and punished by frozen ideas or pampered and loved by bright

objects? Personally, I would rather contemplate the large plaster
hamburger dripping yellow mustard in the sky above
Boy drive-in than worship the pudgy ball of bureauc
above the trees in Bucharest. I'll take a singing hot
red star any day. And then it's a matter of color: (
monochromatic, its predominant color is grey. T
anarcho-chromatic: it aims for tropicalism.

In *Farewell from Nowhere,* a novel by Vladimir
little boy is brought home at night by an old p   ives
inside a hollow metal mountain. Where are v   s the
terrified boy. In His boot, the peddler says   ntly. They are
inside the boot of the giant statue of Stalin that used to straddle
the Volga and Don river.

That Stalin must have been the largest ever produced. In my
childhood, toward the end of the fifties, the official iconography
of the State had reached a "stable" point, meaning that there is a
height and weight beyond which even Stalin couldn't rise
without disappearing from sight. I spent much of that childhood
watching the letters of the sacred name disappear from the
mountain directly across from town. After his death, they had
allowed the trees to grow in the hollows of his name—and year
after year one letter after another became indistinguishable. But
it took years: the *L* alone stretched between my eleventh and
twelfth year.

Another use to which we put the statues was erotic. The large
statues and empty official museums provided ideal places for
young lovers. Lenin, Stalin, and the Communist Party were to
us what the hot leather seats of your cars were to you. In their
shadows, we felt the joy of our adult beginnings. I will never
forget how the bronze wrinkle in the back of Lenin's neck
contracted and expanded with my first love.

A Hungarian friend gave me a treasured piece of metal last
week. It is the size of a quarter. It is also a fragment from the
top button of Stalin's overcoat from the statue the people of
Budapest tore up with their bare hands in 1956. I hold this
talisman dear. It vibrates like a dowsing rod, impossible to
restrain, whenever another statue topples or is about to.

The Burger Genius

Ray Kroc, the genius of the Big Mac, has gone to the Golden Arches in the sky. His was the only business to consciously pursue infinity, to actively hunt eternity. Already, by the time there were One Billion Sold, it was clear that only the national debt could hold a candle to that awesome figure. Five Billion, Six Billion, Seven Billion . . . each year was another proud climb up the rungs of infinity. If anybody in the world's going to heaven, Ray Kroc will.

When I first came to America, my friends were quick to induct me into the cult of McDonald's. Before I could speak a complete sentence, I'd already eaten four Big Macs, and was well on my way to citizenship. When I could understand, my friend Jeffrey Miller, a poet, told me that the Trinity of America was Burgers, Bourbon, and Marlboros—and that if I wanted to thrive I should pay my respects.

Traveling across the continent, I soon learned another secret, namely, that there was no point in leaving home because home was everywhere, identical in every way, especially in food. Gone were all those obnoxious regional differences, those embarassing dialects, the funny food our parents used to make. What the railroad, the radio, the phone, and the TV failed to do, McDonald's accomplished. Had Ray Kroc been a zealot leader, speaking a foreign language and worshipping a savage God, we would have surely risen in arms against him for trying to obliterate our differences. But he was not; he was that brilliant and quintessential figure, the Lone Man With One Idea.

Sure, I have vegetarian friends who grumble on behalf of all the cows. They say that when you die you go to a place where you will be surrounded by all the animals you ever ate, with the parts you ate missing: a chicken with just a wing gone, a cow with a burger taken out of it. That's nonsense. Ray Kroc would see wounded cows everywhere by now if that were true.

McDonald's not only unified us but it civilized us as well. Who can now accuse us of being heartless when, as Jeffrey Miller wrote:

> The Heart is
> A Quarter Pounder.

Brand New World

I found the most beautiful art object of our time on the floor of my friend's car. A can of beer. Not just any can of beer but the ultimate can of beer, a can Andy Warhol would have loved to paint if it had been around when he was painting cans.

I held this can in my hand—with the sense of wonder which only art can inspire—and wrapped my fingers around its comfortable rotundness. The object was perfectly smooth and white. On it, written in bold, black letters was the single word, BEER. How elegant. There was no excess information, no chromatic and offensive assault on my senses. The vulgarity of useless appeals to taste and the apology for incomprehensible content were notably absent. The only other thing written on this can—at the very bottom in very tiny black letters—was:

BY THE GENERIC COMPANY OF AMERICA

Indeed. Here was an object perfectly matched to the intellectual level of its consumer. "Let's get a beer," said to a friend, now meant just that. A beer was finally a beer was a BEER.

Soon after, I found myself contemplating a pyramid at the supermarket. This "generic" pyramid contained only plainly labeled foods. There was FLOUR, COFFEE, SYRUP, BEANS, RICE, and NAPKINS. A sort of blissful simplicity like a breeze of a long-forgotten past wafted from the pyramid. Pyramids, I am told by workers in the Transamerica Corporation's pyramid in San Francisco, keep you forever young. The workers in question have worked there for over a year, and neither one of them has aged a bit. I swear by their peach fuzz. Something similar attended the Generic Pyramid at the Giant. An air, an aura. I stuck my nose into COFFEE. It was good. The pyramid stood there, stark, simple, elegant, and cheap, and it occurred to me, suddenly, that this was the edge of a new world pushing through the earth into ours.

In this new world our limited capacity for making choices is released from its endless bouts with the trivial. No longer will I have to spend agonizing hours in front of multicolored appeals to my strained taste. I remember the agony (which he mistook for ecstasy) experienced by a recent émigré to this country, a friend of mine, when I took him to his first deli. At first, his mind did not accept the randomness of patterns in the meats stretched before his eyes in seemingly endless rows. He was then lost in the cheeses, scattered among the olives, awkward among the breads, hallucinating in the slaws, and emotionally devastated by the variety of sea life on ice. At closing time, the owner and I removed him to a bar where only the realism of five beer glasses brought him back. Luckily, he didn't know what beers they were. To him they were BEER. Needless to say, he has since become calloused and preoccupied like most of us, spending all his time and energy trying to decide among brands. Now all this may be over. He and I may talk again. Over a BEER. Over a hunk of BREAD and CHEESE.

If what I think is true, an extraordinary future brews in and around us. THE GENERIC COMPANY OF AMERICA, whoever they are, have grasped a fundamental truth. Man longs for simplicity. We are now crowded beyond endurance with choices which have little or nothing to do with us. Our language is weighed with the uncertainties of specialized words. Enormous misunderstandings arise from mispronounced technologies. We are force-fed nuance and made schizophrenic by multiplying faces on television. But imagine—if you can—The Generic Future.

Before you do so, however, imagine the *opposite* of The Generic Future: the world of Infinite Choices. In that world you will have to posit yourself a priori in front of any given item and spend your life there. For instance, if you decide on Campbell soup, you will very likely spend your life traveling on shelves between the humblest CHICKEN STARS to the metaphysically bottomless CAMPBELL'S PRIMORDIAL SOUP. Obviously, you wouldn't do much writing, for one thing. If the ever-expanding overspecialized capitalism of our time is allowed to expand unchecked, the world of Infinite Choices looms ahead like a carnivorous TV set. Happily, it won't be. The Generic Pyramids push through the floors of the present.

The Generic Book is already here. There are Generic Romances, Generic Gothics, Generic Sports, Generic Porno. And one day there will be the ultimate Generic Book, the book simply called BOOK. This is the only book you'll ever need, though at first you might buy several, unsure about the content. You need not fear: it will be the same book, every time.

Propped against the Beer, the Book stares at the Man reading it. In the House Next Door, a Woman also reads the Book. They are alone, the only two People in the World, reading their Book. The Star shines on them: the Generic Company of America gives off the Light.

Buying

I hate shopping. I don't know how. In Romania, where I grew up, there wasn't a blessed thing to buy. Compared to Americans, who have master degrees and doctorates in shopping, Romanians are in kindergarten. And personally, I flunked even that. I do not seem to muster the concentration necessary to gaze upon things. In order to shop, you must look at many things carefully, and not only does each thing take time, but things have been getting smaller. There are more, smaller things in the world, and the time it takes to look at each one is staggering. With my terrible training, it takes me a week to get through one isle of the supermarket. A fellow Romanian, a guy I know, was lost in one of those humongous California shopping malls, and hasn't been heard from in a year. Last seen near the River of Shoes, he must by now be in the Sea of Towels, preparing himself to face the Forests of Lingerie. In America, of course, shopping is life. The strongest form of dissent an American can articulate is: "I'm not buying that!" and "that" refers to everything, from an idea to a plan of action. Americans either "buy it" or "don't buy it." When they die, they buy the farm. Though what good is a farm to a dead man, I haven't figured out. In our world today, people do not divide any longer between the haves and the have-nots. Those classes have been replaced by the Bored and the Entertained. The difference between them is the quality of shopping they are able to do. The bored buy cheap and boring things that look the same. The entertained buy expensive and unique-looking things. But I tell you what bothers me most about shopping: it is not very good entertainment. I would rather talk. And you definitely can't shop and talk at the same time. It's like two enemy religions clashing. To a talker, things are a kind of cancer of inarticulation. They pop their pseudodesirable heads in the vacuum left by thought.

Merry Christmas.

Shoe Town

There was one thing in America that you could always be sure of, namely, that signs mean exactly what they say. This was a matter of endless confusion to your average European, used to signs meaning many other things besides what they said. For instance, the sign BUS STOP could mean any number of things in Rome. It could mean that a bus had once gone by and that the sight was now merely commemorative. Or it could mean that the bus stopped halfway up the block if an old woman or an imposing personage flagged it down *over there*. Not so in America. My mother had no end of grief trying to flag the bus down halfway up the block. It never stopped anywhere except where it said BUS STOP. This literalism of American life was exasperating at first, but then a certain kind of comfort came from it. After all, she said, isn't it nice to trust *something*?

But things are changing, alas. The best clothes for my money are not to be found in clothing emporiums these days. They are in shoe stores. Yes, Shoe Town is quietly selling clothes. When the matter of refrigerators came up the other day, I discovered the sturdiest and cheapest at a Michelin Tire place. Restaurants seem to be doing a good business selling T-shirts. Fried chicken joints sell the best fish.

The insidious desire to become someone else, so prevalent among human beings, is beginning to attack the sober world of things. Very soon, BUS STOP will mean the place where you can see that movie. If that.

Of course, I'm a fine one to talk. I'm a Romanian teaching English to Americans. It's a little like bringing coals to Newcastle, or transistors to Japan. But that's life now, going faster than the signs.

Miniotels

I stayed in this Japanese hotel in New York. There was everything: a small refrigerator with complementary sodas, a shower with a shower curtain, a TV set, a writing table, and lots of closets—and all of it could have fit inside a 1950s TV console. Right over my head were lamps, reachable by a half-stretched arm. Likewise the toilet paper, the faucet sink, and the mirror were all where they were logically supposed to be. There was a place for the soap, a place for used razor blades, and a stool for a guest. Had I been a logical creature, I might have been perfectly at ease. Alas. I reached for the light and my hand went through the side of the closet. I turned on the wrong faucet and the shower started. I tried to turn off the shower and I snagged the shower curtain. When the curtain fell it caught the toilet flush and that started the other faucet. I slipped and brought down the towels on top of the TV and the TV toppled on top of the bed, which upset the writing table and sent my papers flying. When I tried to catch my papers, the closets flew open and my clothes flew out of them, so I dropped the papers and tried to chase my clothes, which brought me into the wall and through it into my neighbor's room, a man—or at least I think it was—moaning under a mass of paper, clothes, and soap suds. The impact of my careening pile hitting his relatively stable mound sent both of us crashing through the floor on the room below where we buried a Japanese executive reading the *Wall Street Journal* in front of the TV. His room *had* been pretty neat, I'll say that. By the time we finished moving, we were all in the lobby, screaming at the manager. "What do ya expect?" he said. "In New York? For only seventy-five dollars a night?" Indeed.

I had forgotten. I extricated myself from the mess and vowed to become more efficient. I'm having myself transistorized even as I speak.

Faith in Banks

It astounds me what faith we have in the day-to-day working of our institutions. Even those of us who are rather dubious of their general intentions. When something goes wrong, as it did for me the other day, we simply cannot believe it. What, my bank betray me?

What happened was that I'd sent my bank two deposits by mail. Quite sure that nothing ever goes wrong, I then wrote a check. It bounced. I called the bank. They said the deposits never came. WHAT?? Not possible!

Many years ago, when I first came to America, I would not have been so surprised. Where I come from, things going right is the exception rather than the rule. The same goes for many other countries. Ask a Mexican or an Italian. WHAT, SOME-THING WENT RIGHT? they are apt to ask. They are quite resigned to the breakdown of the machinery on all levels, from the cosmic to the mechanical. In Italy, they find express mail in thistle fields by the roads. In Mexico, a banker will slam a CLOSED sign right in your face after waiting two hours in line. By the same token, he will open the bank for you at midnight if you can tell him a particularly touching story, such as: I'm dying, and if I don't get the money I'll never see my aged mother again!

In this country, however, we just expect things to work. We don't expect them to be human or to care about our mothers, we just expect them to work.

When the bank broke the news to me, my first reaction was to call the FBI. The second was to never trust the system again. I vowed to have myself paid in gold from now on, use no banks, deliver my mail personally, and take no vouchers. But just as I so decided, the bank called. Said they found the money.

OK. But I'm not innocent anymore.

The Wallet

I fell for the wallet gag once, when I was a kid. I saw a wallet on the street, but before I could put my foot down on it, the wallet moved, and a bunch of ruffians giggled me out of the block. I've been weary of "finds" like that ever since, but once in New York it snowed money on me. I was coming home late from a dive, a snowstorm was beginning, and as I took dreamy steps through the fat flakes, five-dollar bills floated down from the heavens on my head. I collected ten before someone more productive gathered the rest. I gave half those bills to the last panhandler on Saint Marks' Place, a kid with a flute frozen to his lips. Since then, my relations to dream cash have been evenly divided between the wallet gag and the cash snow.

In the latest episode, I lost my wall bank card. My secret number was written by me right on it, so I would know what to press when I stood before the wall. Alas, both card and number were gone. I discovered the loss two days later. I gave my checking account a fifty-fifty chance of having made it. If I had lost it on the airplane, it had a sixty-forty chance, because air travelers are affluent. But I'd also been going by bus, so forty-sixty was more like it. I rushed to the first wall with my wife's card and, alas, I'd been right. Yes, my checking account hadn't made it. It had been cleaned down to one buck forty. Instead of dwelling on my loss, I tried to think instead of the lucky finder, who must have thought money snowed on him from heaven. Probably a victim of the wallet gag since early childhood, the hapless bus rider must have felt that the tide was turning. Only trouble is that his tide was turning with my cash. And that's the trouble, anyway you look at it. One man's dream cash is another's nightmare. You can also look at it on a larger scale:

most of us get to be the butt of the wallet gag for most of our lives. While we chase the rigged wallet down the street, somebody's picking *our* wallet out of our back pocket. Or it falls while we run after the gag one. Meanwhile, I stand before the cash wall, wailing.

The Devastated Future

Waverly Elementary School, a beautiful, old building where my son once went to school, is now a twisted heap of rubble. Like most of America's past it will give way to a parking lot. Years from now, he will wander about here, looking for a continuity or a memory and will find what all Americans find when they go back: nothing, a howling emptiness. An ugly, standard, government-issue cement box passes itself as the new school a little ways off. The new building could be anywhere: anonymous, boring, and vague like a gas station or McDonald's, it is distinguished only by its sad reminder of loss.

There is something terrifying about a world that wipes out its past with such greedy speed. The school I went to had been standing for two hundred years or more; and its discomforts, such as drafty classrooms and dim hallways, were made up for by a mysterious and wonderful sense of human continuity, legend, and tradition. A living sense of something both comforting and real whispered to me through the draftiness and the dimness. My childhood unhappiness found secret echoes of others who had somehow gone through here and survived. The shrieking neon anxiety of a new building would have deprived me of something precious and undefinable.

One of the more tragic landscapes of America lies parallel to the railroad tracks between Baltimore and New York. Here, we have the illness and terror of America in its rawest form. The endless, desolate stretches of industrial wasteland give rise to a curious notion: the future is already in ruins. All these industries of the eastern seaboard had once been in the business of the future. They had been producers of things we have barely understood and only vaguely remember, things which were modern, new, futuristic and imbued with the idea of progress. But no sooner did this future appear than it was already obsolete. You feel, passing through the hellish devastation of the Jersey shore, the presence of a ghost, the ghost of the future.

Americans have been running away from their past until there is finally no more place to run to. The great westward migration has stopped at the shores of the Pacific where it has reproduced in exact details all the ills it has supposedly left behind.

There is a poignant scene in more than one American novel, where the hero returns to the past for an understanding of where he or she has been, for an understanding too of who he or she is, and finds nothing. It is a moment worth remembering becasue we all have to do it sooner or later. At that moment, we ask ourselves one of the few questions that really matter. Was it worth it for the sake of the freeway? Was it worth it for the parking lot? The answer has to be no, no matter how many shares you own in the contracting companies: the freeway is old already, the parking lot has weeds growing through it, and there are discarded hypodermic needles by the side of the road.

The argument that sometimes things that are not good for human beings make good business sense, doesn't even hold. The sad thing is that very little of our destructive obsession with progress makes any sense at all.

Time Tracks

_____

From the town of my childhood comes the devastating news that the trolleys are no more. Like my childhood itself, the clanging cars going up the hill past the medieval square to the woods on the edge of town are now relegated to memory, that preposterous and unreliable refuge of things once loved and taken for granted.

The trolley was the joy of that childhood, spent riding on the back of the last car, without a ticket, ready to spring at the slightest sign of the conductor, feeling canny, strong, and free. I used to jump out by the museum where, worn out by the hill, the car slowed down to a lazy crawl. Lazy and still like the hot afternoon and like the car, the town offered itself to my wanderings. I cannot imagine that slow medieval burg without a trolley. (Besides the trolley, Sibiu had had the first gas street lights in Europe and then, exhausted by its effort at modernity, it had settled into a provincial wait of a century.)

In America I was amazed to find the trolley car assigned to nostalgia, regarded as a quaint, antique relic. Since then I have seen the extraordinary speed with which everything becomes old in this country. As I have written elsewhere, America seems to be "an anthology of fads chasing each other faster and faster across shorter and shorter time spans." In a few years I have seen cars, houses, and cities become old, collectible, and misted in legend. Machines created to become instantly obsolete served people whose clothes, hairstyle, and even vocabulary become old-fashioned before my very eyes.

At the increasing rate of this phenomenon, I expect that every human encounter will contain, without any delay, its own past, present, and future. A man, for instance, will, in the course of a sentence, declare his love for a woman, decide that love is futile, and declare that he will never see her again. This, before they have introduced each other. All around them the city will suffer continuous urban renewal, going from brick to glass to cement, from highrises to underground dwellings while the clothes on their bodies will suffer extreme changes of style, so rapid that they will appear to be dressing and undressing continuously as their hair changes color and shape and their eyes narrow and widen to the beat of relentless music.

Such fierce motion will eventually, as it seems to be doing, double up and return to places it had abandoned. In San Francisco, where the trolley car goes and comes back on the wake of tourist desire (the city's desire for tourists and the tourists' desire for the city), one can witness the changes as if on a video screen. The natives are fond of the trolleys, but they will rarely ride them unless possessed by a perverse whim to disguise themselves as tourists. They prefer the buses and the subway. The tourists, on the other hand, feel that they have returned to the past of their own cities where, of course, the trolley tracks have long ago been paved over.

The Russian poet Andrei Voznesensky entitled one of his books *Nostalgia for the Present*. This could only refer to the greed with which we devour the world, and the regret we feel immediately afterwards. In these energy-conscious new times we are suddenly beginning to look with new eyes at things in the not-so-distant past. All the objects residing in our nostalgia are suddenly beginning to shine with the light of utility. We live now at the crossroads of nostalgia and utility, like visitors in a museum which seems unexpectedly more efficient than our own modern house. Like trolley cars, the insufficiently used wonders of our childhood are making the return trip.

Under the asphalt pavements of our city streets, the trolley tracks firmly embedded in cobblestone wait patiently. At night you can feel the ghosts of an energetic, end-of-the-nineteenth-century America crying under its hasty grave.

This is the America Walt Whitman praised, seeing in its

extraordinary technical know-how and its naive but powerful enthusiasm a sign of better times to come. The trains, which more than anything served his vision of a utopia, have practically stopped running. The trolley cars on which the population found itself in a new intimacy going to the theater, the movies, and the lecture hall, went nowhere one day. Was Whitman wrong? It would seem that way.

The trains, panacea of early capitalism, of which the trolley cars were an offshoot like a domesticated species of animal, had an air of gentility and culture about them. Of course, there were also robber-barons and Chinese coolies and murdered Indians. Still, the trains ran on coal which came right out of the ground and on electricity which came right out of the river. They were not controlled long-distance from Arabia.

Whatever happened, happened fast. And whatever is happening is also happening fast. I will not be surprised to wake up one morning to the clanging of trolley bells past my house here in America. The other trolleys, the ones in my childhood, may have to wait, though. They have taken a century to go and, in a slow country like Romania, they may take another to return. Paradoxically then, my childhood in the old country may be waiting for me in the future of my new one.

Nostalgia by Zipcode

We were updating our mailing list prior to keying it into Data Base II, when we suddenly looked at each other. I was in New York and Alice was in California and we both had the same thought. Alice said: "I'm getting nostalgia by zipcode."

There it was. 10009, the zipcode of our youth. The Lower East Side of New York. Poking about inside those zeros like inside mysterious eggs were the younger us. See those two kids hugging each other and themselves in the January wind tunnel of Eighth Street between Fifth Avenue and Cooper Square? Aiming to make it unfrozen to the black cube? That's us, living the bohemian life, live and uncensored.

Alice had her hands on 94110. That was San Francisco. Those two ones are us, walking upright under the impossible blue sky of the city of Saint Francis. The zero at the end is another egg, containing, no doubt, the minute details of the past. In the eggs of those zeros there lives, it seems, the unborn past. Memory is best stored in eggs just like new life. In fact, new life may only be a concentration of memory taking on a new body.

And so it goes. The 48009 of Birmingham, Michigan. Snow, poetry, and small flames of language. And larger flames of burning buildings. And the making of family. The infinity of the 8 concealing in its chambers the upper and the lower projections.

95462. Smell of redwoods. Oxygen. Critical fire index. Sluggish river. And this poem I wrote: "The trees may be scary / but hidden among them / is your house." The smell of autumn. The endless rain. The Bergman festival in the dark Quonset hut by the river. Friends. Lovers. The ocean sunsets in Alice's paintings.

On and on they roll, the zipcodes of our lives, a great river of zeros about to empty into the ocean of Data Base II. The phone rings. It's a fellow editor who would like to buy our mailing list for his publication. "How much?" he says. How much, indeed.

Vacation

I am going to tell you something terrible. I have never taken a vacation.

True, I have lived in places other people take their vacations *to,* but it isn't the same. The idea of a vacation, if I understand it correctly, is to do none of the things you do at home. What avails the man the beauty of oceans if he has to do his laundry in them?

Paradise, after you live in it for a while, is as boring as oatmeal. The natives of Paradise often go crazy and do odd things that amuse the tourists. But no one is a character to himself, whether he lives in heaven or not. What tourist to San Francisco has not found the Golden Gate Bridge immensely more mysterious for the knowledge that unhappy souls jump from it every day? I know one of the few survivors of a leap from that bridge. He told me that he felt terribly uncomfortable knowing that he would turn up in a hundred home movies in the Midwest as he took his leap. This, he told me, is perhaps why he survived.

Stories like that have caused me to take "vacations of the mind" instead. I'll explain. A few years ago, a friend of mine who lived on the east side of town (I live in the west) complained about never getting any mail. That very same evening I wrote him a letter. It was dated *July 10, 1981, Rome.* "Dear Michael," it began, "today I jumped into Fontana Trevi and gathered a pocketful of change." Next day, I received this from *Pamplona, Spain:* "Dear Andrei, Today they let the bull loose on the streets and I barely escaped with my life." Over the next ten months we treated each other with our wild adventures in Madagascar, Macchupichiu, Mauritius, Kathmandu, Venice,

Rio de Janeiro, Port-Au-Prince, Lake Balathon, Odessa, Bahia, Kenya, Madras, Patzcuaro, and places we made up, like Mountain of the Frozen Gold Buddha, Nymph Lake, Heart of the Palm, Mare Nostrum (on the moon), and Mare Tranquilitas (also on the moon).

Our biographers will be amazed at our travels a hundred years hence. Take my word for it, the greatest voyages are made in the mind.

Nomadic Yoga

———————

It's that time again when poets, gypsies, and roving scholars move. Suitcases tied with string, upside-down chairs embracing each other, oddly labeled cardboard boxes with even odder knicknacks inside, table legs, and books pile up on the sidewalks. These urban mountains rise every fall from the pavements of our cities, appearing and disappearing faster than volcanoes. They leave behind bits of strewn debris, an old address fluttering from a napkin or a forgotten letter.

I have moved many times in these past few years and I have come to regard each move as a combination of spiritual rite and madness. The pleasure of getting rid of things is a purge that leaves me cleaner and freer. It is astounding how much junk one collects in the course of a sedentary life.

What need have I of five clocks, three of which don't work? Ideally, I shouldn't need any, but I'm taking one along just in case. And how about all those suits, worn only once, whose very presence makes me feel that I'm perpetually applying for a job? And do I really want this radio with its deafening blasts of advertising and bad news? And this black and white TV filled with the mindlessness of our time? And do I truly want these six cigarette lighters now that I think I've quit smoking?

And even these books here, hundreds of them, most of them unread, what good are they? They have been a millstone around my neck and a postal nightmare ever since I remember. They have followed me around, these bleak tomes, like a faithful herd of cattle. Which ones would I take to a desert island? Three: Whitman, Blake, and Rimbaud. The rest, especially those fat volumes I once planned to read during a hard Russian winter in front of a fireplace, can stay behind. Winters have come and gone and I still haven't read them.

The neighbors won't be sorry to see us go. They may be startled, the way someone is when something familiar isn't there anymore, a mailbox or a tree perhaps. One time, after we had lived for five years in the same house, one of our neighbors came out to watch us loading the truck. "Are you the new people moving in?" he asked. "Yes," I said.

The settled people, who live and die where they were born, will never understand the nomads. They look at us fearfully, making sure their doors and windows are locked. Gypsies, after all, have been known to make off with a clock or a suit or a cigarette lighter or a book. When the settled people, for reasons beyond their control, have to take to the road, they take everything with them. One has to look only at those sad pictures of peasants running away from war with horsecarts loaded dangerously with everything they own, to realize the difference. I need only a satchel and a stick.

I once knew a charming character in Detroit who traveled with two suitcases, one filled with matchbooks, the other with rags. He was as solemn about his rags and matchbooks as sane people would be about their Swiss watches and family heirlooms. When someone asked him what need he had of those things, he looked startled. "Need?" These were *his* things, for better or for worse, what's need got to do with it?

When it comes down to the final decision of what to take and what not to take, I always decide for those things that are the work of someone's hands: paintings, drawings, manuscripts, photographs. Everything else seems useless. After all, we came in the world with nothing and will leave that way. The best we can do in between is to make a few things with our own hands and minds. Buying doesn't qualify as a creative activity.

Children hate to move. The sadness they feel is so great it must be part of the great sadness people felt when they were kicked out of Paradise. Children live so much in the here and now, they cannot bear to see the familiar disappear. Their sadness breaks my heart. I cannot explain to them that the unknown is wonderful, too. I feel some of their sadness as well, because, as the French say: *"Partir c'est mourir un peu"* or "To leave is to die a little." But then again, as Vladimir Nabokov said: *"Mourir c'est partir un peu trop"* or "To die is to leave a little too much," and I often feel that staying in the same spot for too long is a lot more like dying than moving. After all, the dead do not move.

So here we are, sad and giddy, getting rid of things and deciding which ones mean something. This is a healthy, if not entirely happy process, but in the course of it we find ourselves. Moving is a form of soul searching.

Gypsy, Brother

I gave a poetry reading in Boston recently, and a gypsy came up
to me during the intermission and asked to read my fortune. I
have no idea what a gypsy was doing at a poetry reading, but
from my occasional acquaintance with them, there is one thing I
know for sure: Gypsies always pop up where you least expect
them to be.

My first encounter with a gypsy fortune teller was in Romania
when I was ten. She was sitting on the curb in front of our
house, her colorful skirts overflowing, and she grabbed my hand
as I went by. "I see a lot of travel and fame," she said. I was
impressed, not the least by her wild black hair and big, dark
eyes. My mother saved me that time. She threatened to call the
police and the woman went on her way.

When I was growing up, I made friends with some gypsy
kids. Once they had me over for dinner in the gorge outside the
town where they were camping. I remember the smoke from
their open fires drifting sweetly into the sunset. Copper caldrons
with bubbling stews boiled over them. The stuff was delicious.
These gypsies were spoon- and bowl-makers and I ate out of a
new wooden bowl. They also mended things and sharpened
knives. They disappeared all of a sudden one day after a great
number of missing chickens attracted the attention of the
authorities.

In San Francisco one day, we found a crudely printed notice
on the windshield of our banged-up Vega: "If you want dent
fixed, call me and I'll fill it." More curious than hopeful, I called
the number. "I have special cream," the voice on the other end
said, "You put cream in the dent and after five days, boom, the
cream fills hole and it's like new!" I recognized the unmistakable

accent of a Rom. I knew a few bad words of Romany from my childhood, which I then used to great effect. There was an explosion of laughter on the other end and the gypsy insisted that we meet.

We met for a lunch at a Chinese restaurant and I was treated to a great display of gypsy hospitality. My acquaintance was a small, dark man with liquid eyes. He insisted I order only the most expensive things on the menu and lots of it, and then he paid with great flourish. "We gypsies are brothers!" he said, between gales of laughter.

I'd had another taste of gypsy generosity in Rome, years before, when I was introduced to a man named Willy. Willy dressed expensively and he was something of a king, a "boulibasha." His function, as he explained it, was to go to cities in advance of his troop and find out information about available jobs, camping sites, etc. He let it be known with a wink that he also bribed officials where necessary. He was a functional illiterate but he could speak thirteen languages fluently. He treated three of us to dinner, to a nightclub, and to an after-hours place. I didn't see him again, but my friend Marcel struck up a friendship with him and that same year, on Marcel's birthday, Willy gave him a new Mercedes. Marcel didn't know how to drive and he refused the car. Willy was mortally offended and he drove the Mercedes away himself, straight into a telephone pole. Marcel visited him next day in a hospital.

There were gypsy storefronts in San Francisco (for some reason they never live above the ground floor) and I used to study their contents with amusement. Among cheap plaster representations of madonnas with child and dried flowers there were such items as ceramic nymphs and old issues of *The New Yorker*. Sometimes at night, the curtains were not drawn and I could see large families with many children sitting around tables with empty wine bottles. The remarkable thing seemed to be that the children looked as wide awake as if it had been 10 A.M. Outside, parked at various odd angles were station wagons and vans with license plates from as far away as Maine.

Gypsies say that in the beginning of the world all people were gypsies. God gave them a stone to keep and take care of but they lost it. From that day on, gypsies have been roaming the world over looking for that stone. When they find it, all people will be gypsies again. A simple enough religion.

But my favorite gypsy story has to do with the violin. It seems that in a village there was a young girl (not a gypsy) who wanted to win the heart of a young man. She asked the devil to help her and the devil gave her the violin in exchange for her soul. She played it and won her young man but on the day of her wedding, the devil came and took her. She dropped the violin and a gypsy who was passing by picked it up.

In our stable and worried world, we may take heart from the gypsies. They may be a little crooked, but they are still looking for something and they can make heartbreaking music.

Psychointersections

The first time I went to Boston, the poet John Weiners gave me a tour of his city. But he didn't take me to City Hall or the Fish Market. Instead, he took me to modest streets here and there. He said, "This is where Charles Olson first told me that he liked my poetry." And later, at another obscure intersection, at a small store between two houses, he said, "That's where I bought Bob Creeley a lemon meringue pie." And so it went, John's personal Boston, unmarred by the grandeur of sanctioned history.

The other day I was wandering in my home town, another fine ground for memories, and came upon the following intersection, dear to me: MELVILLE & FRISBY. This is where I first lived when I came here, and I remembered just how important this intersection became. I considered the conjoining of those names a fortunate and splendid sign. Of course, the Melville they had in mind was not Herman Melville, but an obscure local politician. And Frisby was spelled with a *y* not two *e*'s, the way you spell that lovely flying object. Small details, however, because those two names expressed clearly everything I was about at that time: I aspired to the density and intensity of Herman Melville crossed with the lightness and freedom of a frisbee thrown by a coed on a college campus green in, let's say, 1975. And that's the way I lived under that sign. I even wrote a newspaper column named "Melville & Frisby."

I realized then that all cities have these nodes, these important intersections. I found, one day, Narcissus & Labyrinth. Now, that is a beautiful and seductive sounding pair of streets, though it would be mighty sad living under their sign. Most of humanity, whether it knows it or not, does in fact live under the sign of Narcissus & Labyrinth. Those names are the key to modern existence. And then there was Winner & Gist, not far from Narcissus & Labyrinth. Powerful joggers, power-mad people must live here.

I baptized these seemingly random places, psycho-intersections, for the hidden meanings they carry. They are everywhere. Look around.

Being There

I have a knack for "being there."

In 1978, in Rome, I was two blocks away from Via Caetani, where Aldo Moro's body had been left by his murderers. A silent stream of people pulled me suddenly to the spot when the shocking news broke. A Jesuit priest was leaning over the body, with his rosary.

I felt then like an unwelcome intruder, a tourist with a stupid camera, tramping loudly through other peoples' grief, especially when my son, who was seven at the time, asked me what was the difference between a tourist and a terrorist and I couldn't tell him. Later I thought a tourist is a terrorist with a camera, a terrorist a tourist with a gun. Both rush through landscapes, real or imagined, geographical or ideological, with great speed, blinded by guides or tracts.

On Monday, December 8, 1980, I was teaching poetry to inmates in the Bellevue Prison Ward in New York. The place is a sprawling monster, lit up day and night, like New York, whose craziness it absorbs and safeguards.

The workshop was sponsored by INCISIONS, a non-profit idealistic organization. It went well, considering that the room we were in was lime green in bright white neon and the people seated in the hard red plastic chairs were in various stages of pain.

A man wheeled a steel device with an I.V. bag that attached to his arm and followed him everywhere. Another came in a bed with half his body in a cast and another was obsessively reciting dirty ditties *sotto voce*. A tall black man recited for us what seemed to be the entire philosophy of some obscure mystical sect, rhymed in severe couplets throughout, but was wheeled out of the room in mid-recitation suddenly by Big Sister, whose crisp white uniform preempted all objection.

In spite of this, poetry was very much at home here and I felt, as I read my poem, a huge empathy going from me to those people along a deep fault line, a crack which divided them from society and from themselves, a crack which runs also through poetry and poets if they are any good.

At 10 P.M. it was all over and I wondered, as I headed for the pleasures of food, drink, and music, how much of my empathy had been purely symbolic. I was free and they were not. I was happy, they were in pain. At 10:45 P.M. as I sat in a little restaurant, Chapman shot John Lennon, and at 11:15 P.M. he was brought to the Bellevue Prison Ward for psychiatric testing.

Chapman, whose name really means "nobody" ("chap" is "man," so "man-man" or "nobody") was Lennon's double, a failed double with a gun. He often signed Lennon's name instead of his own, he had a Japanese wife just like Lennon. But for all that, Lennon remained a symbol to Chapman. Chapman was poor, Lennon was rich. Chapman couldn't make music, Lennon did. Frustrated by the unwillingness of the symbol to transform him, Chapman aimed his gun at the man, hoping to kill the symbol. What he did was kill the man and make the rest of us symbol-sick.

Symbols are like travel brochures: They permit you to delude yourself that you know where you are, when in reality you are allowing the symbols to do your thinking for you. A lot of human beings die in the crossfire between symbol-crazy people. We often forget, in our cinematic view of the human panorama, that those flags waving up there are just pieces of cloth.

Chapman was shooting at an image created by record companies and a myth-making culture. The personality cults of the 1970s were all symptoms of our inability to see clearly in an increasingly manipulated forest of symbols. We identified with movie stars, sports figures and pop heroes because it was easier to go for the brightly lit landmarks than to go off the road to explore on our own.

"Insanity," said Nietzsche, "is a rare thing in individuals but habitual to groups, nations and races." Insanity, the insanity that has been killing so many great people in the last two decades, possesses all of us when we allow symbols to grow monstrous, collective, and unchecked.

As the news bulletins in the little restaurant kept coming fast I had a sudden recollection: It was in this very place, twelve years before, that I'd heard, probably from the same radio, the news of Bobby Kennedy's death.

This is the sort of coincidence that makes you wonder if you are not somehow a guest, invited invisibly, to these grisly gala events of death, to witness yet another generational marker. My generation has been marking its passage by these means, having come of age with John Kennedy's murder. But it is precisely this sort of thinking, this easy symbolic manner that you must resist. So you go on eating.

Autumn

In California, where the future is a full-time business, Autumn doesn't come. There are intimations of it in San Francisco, hints of it here and there, a smell traveling and surviving a long journey across the mountains, a few leaves deigning to fall, but in the main the melancholy and pleasure of this season are out of bounds to the inhabitants of paradise.

Autumn cornucopia, its huge horn of plenty discharging its miracles of color, ripeness, and texture on us, is an exclusive reward for having suffered the steamy hells of summer and the winter still ahead. This is a time to consider the notion of the soul and its earthly journey.

"Never was Autumn so beautiful / to our death-happy soul," said the poet Arghezi, in my awkward translation. Death and life, seen briefly in the light of this season, return to us what little of the metaphysical survives in our arid modern psyche. The falling leaf and the ripe fruit illuminate our condition. A happy sadness, a bitter sweetness. This is a time of reconciled paradox and unmediated insight.

In the absence of rotting plenty and sweet sorrow, the natives of sunny climes must be somehow incomplete, like those people who, Pablo Neruda once said, have never tasted peaches. "People like that," said the poet, "would be quietly getting sadder, noticeably paler and, probably, little by little, they would lose their hair."

Here in the city, where buildings stand for hills and people often strike treelike poses and rustle their leaves at intersections, Autumn is even more spiritual than in the countryside. Bared to essences of light, cloud, and wind, it reveals itself starkly and deeply. A swirl of leaves in the path of an incoming bus speak directly to the heart. What heart? you might well ask. I don't know: at the bottom of the homogenized compost heap of life lived in the pale blue rays of television, there beats something. It might be a heart.

For all those who are missing Autumn these days, I append a falling walnut to these speculations.

Autumn's Lament

A sadness invades me every fall. Melancholy of things dying. The proximity of yet another winter. The arctic winds, already blowing, chill the house. They say the trade winds are changing, volcano ash blankets the upper atmosphere, and man-made pollution is killing the ozone layer. All those things mean shorter summers, fiercer winters. A long, polar night waits.

Every fall for the past five years, we've moved. The whole family, bundles of string-tied belongings on our backs, took to the road and found a new place to hole up for the winter. This gypsy streak was usually a cheerful occasion, a way to put off the stillness and the chill, the premonitions of doom, and the mad thought that we might not, after all, be immortal. Students, gypsies, rovers, wanderers, and plain restless people move in space to avoid and deny time. As long as you move, you are alive.

This autumn I find myself contemplating the stillness. There is nowhere to go right now. I envy the birds, their V flocks headed south, where they won't have to worry about the falling peso. Should I imitate them, I would most certainly have to worry about it. They don't look kindly on Americans in Mexico right now. Central America is in the grip of a mortal terror. Farther south, more trouble. Economic uncertainty. Huge inflation, unemployment. Even golden, sunny Florida isn't what it used to be. Things are bad on the ground these days. The world is getting older, meaner, stiller.

Some of us, myself most of all, are pathetic anachronisms. Not so long ago, a sense of optimism and expectancy pervaded the world. I felt that I was living through great changes, that a golden age was around the corner, that people could be simple and human again, as in books or in parts of California on certain days. But I was sorely mistaken. The great changes turned out to be antihuman, not human. Conformity, lack of imagination, pettiness, avarice, and fear are the order of the day. Machines and machinelike people are what's in, for better or for worse, and anyone who doesn't fit their narrow, machined contours is out of joint. If anyone still thinks it's all right to be human, take a look, please, at the arms race and the callous disregard of governments for people. Even the shred of hypocrisy that required a humanistic rhetoric to go with the tightened screw is gone now.

Stendhal, the great French writer, after having lived through the turbulent but hopeful early years of the nineteenth century, which ended at Waterloo, found himself in middle age totally alone, in a strangely conservative world, in a restored monarchy where all his unbelieving, liberal, Jacobin, democratic ideas were suspect and downright subversive. Without making too much of the literary parallels, that's just how I feel, only things are worse now. Stendhal's Bourbons had no atomic weapons.

Pessimism is the chief sentiment of autumn. It goes with the impossibly ripe fruit in the markets and all the plenitude that shines inside it for contrast. In past autumns, I experienced the turn of seasons with pleasure mixed in with the melancholy. This year, I don't know what's wrong. The bad shape of the world doesn't entirely account for it. Maybe it's what the Romanian poet Tudor Arghezi said: "Never was Autumn so beautiful to our death-happy soul." Maybe we experience our mortality in stages, feeling just a little more peculiar each fall until, with a great shudder of regret, we turn into ash. Whatever the reasons, political or existential, or both, this is the . season for poetry. Poetry comes to life of itself now, and if there were no poets to write it, it would write the poets.

I won't leave you like this. Children don't feel this way. The excitement of returning to school hasn't entirely faded yet and the world is still new for them. But their sweetness is only more grist for my melancholy mill. What kind of world are we bringing them up in? With the exuberance of childhood on my left and the worries of my own parents on my right, I am at midpoint between ages. Fall is a fine symbol for all that. Someone said that "middle age is when your parents become your children." That might be it. And the man also said, speaking strictly between men, as we strolled on the college campus, "You know you're getting old when the girls' mothers look better to you than their kids." I like that guy. He calls the shots straight.

After all, this may be a fall like any other, though I doubt it. It may be that I am a sentimental fool. I should be looking at what is with a colder eye. In a colder world, outside as well as inside, the answer might be a little adaptation. Which is to say, a little giving in. Which is to say, a little dying.

Poets' Graves

Every winter I visit the graves of poets. In Paris, a few years ago, I went to the tomb of Guillaume Apollinaire, the great poet of the modern age. It was a pilgrimage many poets have made. On his tombstone is engraved one of his poem-pictures in the shape of a heart: MON COEUR PAREILLE A UNE FLAMME RENVERSÉE, "MY HEART LIKE AN UPSIDE-DOWN FLAME." The Père-Lachaise cemetery, where he is buried, is a city of the famous dead. Marcel Proust is the poet's neighbor. Not far is Honorée de Balzac. It was a cold winter day but I was not alone. All my literary heroes were there. And the cats, the eternal cats of Paris, were flitting among the graves of the patchy snow.

The year after that, I found myself at the graveside of John Keats in Rome, in February. I was there for different reasons but I could not go without paying my respects. The lyre-shaped tree behind his tombstone was bare. It was a mild winter. I read, once again, the words I knew by heart: "This Grave contains all that was mortal of a YOUNG ENGLISH POET who on his death bed in the Bitterness of his Heart at the Malicious Power of his Enemies, Desired These Words to be Engraven on his Tombstone: Here Lies One Whose name is Writ in Water. February 24th 1821."

And this year, again, I found myself visiting Walt Whitman in Camden, New Jersey. Whitman designed his own grave. It is a massive monument made from five slabs of granite. On top of the four slabs that make the little house stands a fifth, a pyramid of rough, chiseled texture. Like the rest of it, the pyramid is of one piece, expressing a great density and weight of purpose. And yet for all its massiveness, it does not seem heavy. There is a lightness in the feeling of the monument, a slight resemblance to an ocean vessel, or to Whitman's own mercurial, open, rolling verse. It is a powerful place to visit on a cold winter day. Something in the granite harmonizes with the sky, and there is, in the severe barrenness of the trees, more than a hint of eternity.

And then it occured to me that in the winter there is a magical and dark moment which only the graves of poets can inhabit.

Hibernation Rumination

This has been a Russian winter, one of those deep Siberian winters when you write long epic novels and stare anxiously at your fire for fear the last log may be burning out. Outside, the wolves are howling and the mailman has disappeared, buried in a snowdrift a thousand miles from here.

This is also the winter you have been thinking about when you said: "I think I'll read *War and Peace* and the *Collected Dostoevsky* one mean winter when I'm old." Well, you may not be old, but here is that winter. This is the winter also of a terrible discontent.

I spent my childhood in the mountains so I know what it feels like to stare dreamily, for many magical hours, at the flowers the frost makes on the glass panes. Sometimes I think my whole childhood passed like that, staring at wintry flora. Whatever poetry I was lucky to write has its possible origin in that timeless dreaming.

I probably saw in those windows the shape of life to come and all the things that have happened in the world since. The enchantment didn't leave me room to remember consciously any of that, but who knows if at some level, I did not turn all that into poetry.

I remember, too, the skeleton of a sea horse someone had brought me one summer. Looking at it in the winter gave me the strangest sensation, as if two impossible climates and geographies meshed in my room.

In California, I started forgetting about winter. They have five seasons there: Drought, Flood, Mud, Fire and Earthquake. None of those has much poetry in it and it only snowed once. I lived sixty miles north of San Francisco, on the Russian River, and the snow was so unexpected and out of place, it startled everything that lived.

The enormous redwoods, overwhelmed by the whiteness and unused to the weight, began to crack and fall on houses, cars, power lines, and each other like big clumsy dinosaurs. It was like the end of the world. Every utility stopped working. The people stared and stared. The river rose in the banks and flooded the town.

This winter is the coldest in Europe in this century. NATO and the Russians are keeping up with it by making Cold War noises. In the bitter cold in Poland, people line up to buy food under the shade of freezing-cold gun barrels.

Winter and war have been wedded to each other in our memories for time immemorial. Who could forget those pictures of hunger and misery in the bitterness of winter in Hitler's occupied Europe, the snows of besieged Leningrad, the rag-tag armies of Napoleon coming back from Russia, George Washington's crossing of the frozen Delaware?

Winter is the season of true war, war unprettied by patriotic, nationalist propaganda, war that cuts to the bone. Since it is also the season of reflection, when we are lucky enough to be at peace, it is a good time to think on the world.

I do my best thinking when I cook. Cooking is a good way to keep warm and soup is the best thing to cook. I love to work on my favorite potato soup as the snow piles up outside and the world gets worse. There is something in the alchemical magic of cookery in the middle of the snow that sends me back to the cave days.

I feel the weight of the heavy bear fur on my back and I like to make short, guttural noises. We would be undoubtedly much better off if we had retained our fur instead of becoming smooth and vulnerable like plucked chickens.

Bring about 15 peeled potatoes and a large chopped onion to a boil in a big pot. Add sliced carrots, green garlic, leek. Fry ½ pound of bacon in a pan with lots of pepper and paprika. When the bacon is crisp, add flour and stock from the soup and turn it all into the pot. When the potatoes are cooked, mix the yellows of 2 eggs in a cup of sour cream with some chopped dill and turn these into the soup. Cook 15 minutes and eat with black bread and butter. I thought you wanted to know.

I don't envy my friends in Bermuda right now. They will look silly when they return, with all that cultivated tan skin, full of the easy babble that comes with those tall rum drinks. They will feel out of place here when we are brooding, serious, dug in, thoughtful, possibly profound.

The Tourist

I hail from a city of towers. The lasting memories of my childhood revolve around the towers of my medieval burg in Eastern Europe. I loved watching them at all hours of the day, but they were best of all at twilight when the setting sun elongated their shadows until they went right through my heart. I think of them sometimes as huge knitting needles at work on the tapestry of my past.

There was the tower of the old Gothic cathedral in the Center Square, a massive fantasy in stone, begun at the onset of the first millennium and finished 350 years later. The gold scales of its roof and the rough-hewn black stones of its severely ascending body were always in front of my window.

There was also a mysterious medieval ruin, fallen onto the wall of an overgrown garden near my house. This had once been a powerful tower, and I spent many hours balancing precariously on the garden wall trying to find a way to enter it. I never did.

And then, on top of my elementary school, which had once been an Ursuline monastery, there was a massive fortress tower with several moss-covered cannon balls still half-embedded in its body. I think the old stones had stood through three Turkish sieges and one surprise attack from Vlad the Impaler.

I often think of writers who grew up among towers. Franz Kafka, for instance, whose old Prague probably resembles my more modest, provincial Hermanstadt. Or Sigmund Freud and Robert Musil in Vienna. I am sure that there is a direct and unequivocal relation between the destiny of these writers and the towers of their native places. Maybe it is only the simple upward thrust of a building straight into the sky, expressing the longing of humans for the miraculous. Or maybe a tower is, as Proust called it, "the finger of God," and the writers follow, naturally, the imperative of its point. Whatever it is, poets and towers are made for each other.

The inhabitants of towers must have been brooding people or maybe not people at all. I sometimes imagine a convention of all the denizens of lighthouses, prisoners of ruined towers and princesses-saved-in-the-nick-of-time and I am scared into poetry.

Of course, not all towers need be gravely serious. One of my favorites is a comico-serious tower on Roland Avenue, in Baltimore. I don't know its name or its purpose but I like to call it Tour Saint Jacques, after the favorite tower of the French Surrealist poets. The original Tour Saint Jacques in Paris is said to throw a purple shadow and have no practical use besides pleasing the poets. Baltimore's Tour Saint Jacques stands there, looking vaguely Italian and content, in a manner that is both idiotic and charming. I would be much surprised to discover that it has a practical purpose. Personally, I hope it doesn't and it stands forever.

City Lights

Huntingdon, Pennsylvania.

The grizzled old farmer on my left leaned over and whispered hoarsely: "Potatoes!" "Pardon me?" I moved my beer glass and looked at him. He shook his head sadly but firmly: "Potatoes!"

A short time later, the man's twin came in and took the stool on my right. Same grizzly chin, greasy overalls, toothless grin. "Onions!" he exclaimed. "Potatoes!" reiterated the one on my left. "Onions!" came the twin's breathless reply.

I decided this had to be a famous local routine. A stranger comes to town, the two comedians sit on each side of him and say "potatoes" and "onions" until the person forks over his assets. But I soon became aware of the rhythm's slacking off and the two of them turned on me simultaneously with the rest of the story.

"Beets!" "An' parsley!" "Parsnips an' carrots!" "Everything with a root!" "'Cept for peas!" "My Pa would plow 'em in just about now!" "An' celery!" Two beers later I was weighed down with planting hints like a human *Farmer's Almanach*.

Outside, I squinted into the sun and took stock of my surroundings. You can see all of Huntingdon, Pennsylvania, from in front of the bar. Blue ridges ring the town with snow still on them. Where the main street stops, the wilderness begins and it doesn't let off until Ithaca, New York.

When students are home on vacation, black bears come on campus; they sleep in the dormitories and turn the record players on real loud. During hunting season, armies of yellow-clad Americans invade the town and kill seven thousand deer at once. They drag the carcasses through the main streets, leaving trails of blood and beer. Except for the black bears and the hunters, things are pretty quiet for the most part. Crime is non-existent, that is, it *was* nonexistent until I got here. Two days after I got here someone robbed the bank. I was asleep at the time, but the town still hasn't gotten over it.

"We don't have the problems you have in the big cities," my host told me. "The air is pure, housing is cheap, prices are good, the folks leave their doors unlocked."

I took a walk through town at night. Everybody was watching TV with their doors unlocked and they seemed to be good. They had to be, all the bars were shut down and there was a church at the end of each street. The only business open, THE QWIKEE STOP, was so brightly lit my shadow fled as soon as I entered.

The State Liquor Store, which I'd visited earlier, also had its bright lights trained on the sinner. The warden, I mean the vendor, stood behind a blinding neon counter flanked by a sample of every kind of liquor offered, all arranged in strict rows with big signs under each bottle in case you missed the labels. After I read the sign and proffered my wish, he went through a door into a dark room. He spent a long time in there, so long I was certain he was conversing with the police computer. Finally, he brought out a bottle. "This time," his gestures implied, "you got away." In Pennsylvania, students tell me, you need something called an LCB card to drink. It stands for the Liquor Control Board, and you apply for it by mail from Harrisburg. You enclose your birth certificate and wait about three months. The town is full of thirsty orphans.

The college sits on top of a hill and all the kids wear T-shirts and parkas with the name of the college on them in case anybody might mistake them for townies. The townies don't wear T-shirts that say "townie." They just drive their pick-ups real fast up the main drag on campus. The kids play their stereos real loud just like the black bears and stomp their feet equally loud on the floor (which is my ceiling). They are good kids, you can tell just by looking at them.

Here is an entry from my notebook, a week after I came:

"Good girls, good folk, good air, good prices, good thoughts—
GOOD GOD!" Being good is very cheap. If you stay home,
watch TV, and use your coupons when you go shopping, there
isn't much to be extravagant with. Even being a little "bad" is
very cheap because of all the surrounding goodness. A drink at
the bar is only seventy-five cents and the potato lecture is gratis.
Walking from one end of the town to the other takes fifteen
minutes and it's free. And I used to think Baltimore was dull!

Many of the students come from even smaller towns. I asked
them, in class, how big their home towns were. It turned into a
contest to see who came from the smallest one. It was won
hands down by a girl who said she came "from a little house in
the middle of a cornfield somewhere." That image nearly drew
tears from me, quintessential city boy that I am. A little house.
In a cornfield. Somewhere. The night must be awesome out
there. I imagined billions of stars and how that far-off train
whistle must sound to the sleepless inhabitant of that place.

I heard a train whistle, too. It was about midnight, and ten
minutes away was THE QWIKEE STOP. I bought a magazine and
an orange soda.

The Earth Shuttle

Huntingdon, Pennsylvania.

Spring is making the students stretch. Listening to the same instructions that make the grass shoot fiercely upward and the leaves race up and down branches and the buds pop, they stretch on lawns behind dormitories and in class and wherever they happen to be. I see them stretched out on the tongues of rock that jut a hundred or so feet over the Juniata River valley. The roar of the river below and the glare of the railroad tracks combine with the clouds to make spaceships of these rocks. I imagine the young people stretched there flying on these tongues of rock over the blue and green ridges, into the wild blue yonder. Space shuttle imagery weaves through college spring.

It is fair time in Amish country, all around us. To get to Belleville, where the fair is, you take a winding road past large, clean Amish farms. You can tell them from other farms because no electric wires go to them. In the fields you see five-horse teams roped to ploughs behind which black-hatted, bearded men, who would look very much at home in a van Gogh painting, walk slowly and firmly.

An unbelievable peace pervades the scene, as if you had been suddenly transported to another time and place, a place that never existed, except ideally, in books, in dreams. Tolstoy's Russia, Brueghel's Holland, Dürer's Germany. On the eve of the shuttle flight, here were these people living by candlelight, refusing to use machinery, rejecting the easy solutions of the world around them. The very conservative among them, who drive home-hewn white wagons, make everything they need by hand. They make their own shoes, their own clothing, their own bread. They are pacifists and they believe in God.

The fairgrounds are drenched in spring sunlight, and throngs of children swarm between tables laden with shoefly and moon pies, elderberry jellies and currant butter. In a low wooden building they are auctioning butter, eggs, and sausage. One carton of big brown eggs for thirty-five cents. The smell of sauerkraut and pork in the air reminds me of my hometown in far off Transylvania, which, like its near namesake state here, was settled by ancient Germans. My colleague, with an innocent air, persuades me to try the shoefly pie. I do and the effect is the same, I remember, as the first time I tried peanut butter. I couldn't open my mouth for one long minute and I thought I was about to die. This is what it must feel like being lowered into a molasses pit.

In the other auction house, where animals are waiting to be sold, a seemingly idle crowd shuffles back and forth. The Amish women, dressed in clean black and blue cloth, carry babies clad much the same way, their faces covered with kerchiefs. They speak a soft Dutch German which I strain to hear, but I can make out very little even with my near perfect knowledge of five Saxon words. The men, some of whom wear one black sus- pender, and some of whom sport two, talk softly among themselves, nodding often. This business of the suspenders, I am told, has to do with a doctrinal difference. Some wear no suspenders at all, trusting to their proud, round bellies to hold up their trousers. The colors of their wagons—white, yellow, and black—point also to differences of religious practice. But whatever those differences, they are friendly and relaxed with each other and with strangers as well, talking easily with anyone who addresses them. One young couple, the woman in her late teens, her red-bearded husband no more than twenty-one, exchange long, funny looks of complicity whenever they speak to someone. She rocks a sleeping baby. They are so much in love they light up the place.

On the bulletin board there are absorbing notices of public sales. You can get a broad selection of Herefords, Holsteins, Anguses, and crosses, varying in weights from 200 to 700 pounds; if you care to pick them up and you have the cash. If that doesn't suit you, how about several good litters of feeder pigs? No room in your yard for them? How about some lambs and a couple of roosters? Here is something I would most certainly enjoy: 3,000 bales of straw and alfalfa. Something akin to nostalgia sweeps over me. Wouldn't it be nice to live up here on a farm, surrounded by animals, in close touch with the earth, watching things grow? It seems like a beautiful way of life from my city perch. But I'm sure I must be forgetting a few things. Things like back-breaking work and the economy. No matter, it's fun to dream.

On the way back from the fair, having purchased a small oil lamp (the kind Diogenes carried around looking for an honest man) and three pairs of 1950s early plastic sunglasses (all I could afford), I feel wistful. How long can these people survive the onslaughts of the space age? Will they be able to keep their children from going away? All they have against it is custom and proud difference. Are those sufficient against the rising price of land and the pressure of development?

On the highway, in front of us, there are several horse-drawn buggies. We pass them. The signs on the sides of the road are like a serial novel: They tell a story from the scriptures. "Prepare to die," one billboard proclaims. "After life, what?" asks another. A few hundred yards after that, the answer: "The Judgment." The questions like the answers unfold gradually, and they are not simple.

Zen and the Second Week of Trout Season

Huntingdon, Pennsylvania.

They say President Carter used to fish this stream for trout, becoming occasionally so absorbed that he lost sight of the man with the "football" shadowing him from the bank. The "football" contains the buttons that can blow the planet to smithereens in case the Russians attack or the man carrying it trips on a root and falls face down on it.

The stream itself is wild, majestic and full of rainbows, steelheads, and occasional pinkos. It is hard to imagine a more incongruous setting for the "football": wild woods in tender spring green, swampland with bright yellow flowers, fallen logs, swift currents, white water, a fine mist in the air.

Should you keep walking east of here you would encounter hundreds of species of birds, wild animals, deep woods and— Three Mile Island. It is the great perversity of our time to set the most potentially evil objects of man in the heart of paradise. Think of all the unsuspecting wild burros in Arizona and New Mexico chewing the primeval weeds on the perimeter of a ghost train for atomic missiles. And think, too, of the Alaskan and the Soviet Eskimos who used to travel a short distance on the Arctic ice to visit each other and who now stare at bristling warheads and acres of blinking radar lights so much stranger than the Aurora Borealis.

I think of all these things as I look at the swirling stream. Fishing is a good sport for presidents because streams tend to suggest such thoughts. The ancient Chinese poet Li Po, who fell into the reflection of the moon on water and drowned in it, thought the same thoughts, too, even though evil in his day consisted mostly of mad emperors who decreed the destruction of history. Those emperors, like most of us, didn't fish nearly enough.

I am fishing for all I am worth but I really don't know the first thing about it. My friends, who invited me so casually, became transformed the instant we reached the stream. From out of the trunk of their car came enormous rubber boots and waterproof vests with hundreds of pockets full of hooks, worms, lures, weights, matches, and scaling knives. The day, too, changed suddenly. At first it had been overcast and misty, now there were intermittent bursts of rain and gusts that wrinkled the water. Each of them had two fishing rods in each hand. I had only one and my temporary seven-day tourist license which had cost me nine bucks and was wrapped in a plastic baggie and safety-pinned clumsily to my borrowed cap. But I was ready to outfish them all.

Suddenly, everyone dispersed, taking off in search of the perfect pool, and I was left by a bend next to a mossy old log just perfect for sitting on and I thought: What am I going to do if I hook a fish? Getting the worm twice through the hook and disposing of the brown goo that shot out of its tubular person was disturbing enough. Sissy city stuff, I admit. But I had nothing to worry about as I soon saw plainly. The fish knew exactly how to eat the worm without getting hooked.

Reeling in the empty hook was a mixed proposition: I loved to cast off as far as I could over the water but then there was the worm. Like everything else in life these days, the simple plea-sures come threaded with gore.

And the pleasures of casting off were further clouded by the fact that twice in a row I caught a tree. The first tree graciously bent to give me back my hook but it kept the worm. The second tree wasn't so nice: It kept my hook and a good part of the line. The rain came down hard at that very moment. I saw one of the fellows I'd come with, far in the middle of the river, fly casting rapidly. I watched with wonder the swift pantomime of his hands.

Fishing is more like Zen than any other kind of meditation. In

Zen things are and are not. When you begin the study of Zen, an old *koan* says, rivers are rivers and fish are fish. During the study of Zen, rivers are not rivers and fish are not fish. I was definitely in the midst of my study of Zen. The river was not a river, it was a source of thought, eddies of energy suggesting themselves to everyone from Li Po to President Carter. And the fish, well, the fish . . . All my fancily appointed friends were tricked by the fish. The fish were not fish, they were silvery, striped demons. In fact, fishing was not fishing. It was Zen.

The fancy lures failed and the murdered worms hung limply. But like the hardy souls we were, we continued our work until the cold began to blow to our bones and cut close to our insides. Slowly, we reeled ourselves through the mud back into the car. Around a bend in the road, not far from this spot, was a country bar. A shot of whiskey flowed warmly into my wet self. Yes, I whispered to myself, I have found my form of leisure. Six days left on my seven-day license.

In the freezer of my friends' icebox were yesterday's trout. Still beautiful in their frozen state, a steelhead, a rainbow, and a golden waited to become dinner. They became a great pleasure in the mouth, indeed, and with that the river became a river again and fish, fish. Only the "football," looming ghostly somewhere about the edges of my mind, did not fit anywhere.

Under Cover

I've been thinking about packages. The art of wrapping is an ancient one. In Japan, people go to school for years to master a hundred ways to wrap an egg. Of course, one couldn't carelessly unwrap something so carefully wrapped. Do people go to school to learn how to *unwrap* things? No. For the Japanese, the package is the whole statement. Inside, there is only a pretext.

Not so with us, who tear blindly through anything in order to find the center, the meat, the essence. No nakedness is naked enough. The *real* thing must be deeper inside, dig? The brutalized wrappings lay strewn about us, the mile-deep debris of our hunger for things.

For all that, America makes the most astounding packages in the world. A short trip through the cereal isle in the supermarket can take your breath away like an alpine Swiss vista. Our packaging isn't unlike Japanese art: it, too, is an art of the exterior, attaching little or no importance to what's inside. I have yet to find a cereal that tastes as good as it looks. For a measure of how we are becoming more Japanese, it suffices to look at my friend Mary's family. Her grandfather made a fortune inventing a bread-wrapping machine. Her father designed the individual cereal pack, that stylized wonder of solo living. Mary herself is a master of origami, the Japanese art of paper objects. In three generations, utilitarianism gave way to esthetics.

A package containing a surprise is always interesting. But when the package itself is the surprise, a whole revision of values must take place. We must forsake greed for beauty. Try telling children that. Occasionally though, a huge package comes along that changes our whole idea of content. The Bulgarian-born artist Christo wrapped up the Empire State Building. When he wrapped an Australian beach in tinfoil, the natives cried. A present on such a scale is almost inconceivable, never mind that you already know what's inside. Christo's packages make a great mystery out of the familiar, and they suggest as well that *everything* can be transformed. Even the megalomaniac wishing to present the night sky to his love can find a way.

It is good to remember as well that everything *is* a package. The most intriguing, only partially known, and always surprising, is the human body. Artfully wrapped in skin, it is the supreme package.

Thin Ice

Everybody I know has a disaster scenario for the late 1980s, a sort of garden of doom in the middle of which flowers The Crisis.

An oil shortage leading to World War III was a great favorite for a while. It was simple, almost elegant, and everything could be made to fit into it: inflation, unemployment, instability, conflict.

Then the Oil Issue moved to the side to make room for the New Continental Drift Theory. The struggle in the United States and Canada between the industrialized, clumsy, overstructured East and the resource-rich, informal West; and between the cold North with its attached moral fiber (it takes guts to survive in Jack London's prose) and the sunny South, lush, eccentric, and cheap.

Parallel but not unrelated (a sort of ideological maiden aunt returning from exile in Orange County) was the Communist Menace. Uncomplicated by the subtleties of its younger kin, The Menace sees the Soviets advancing, the Americans standing firm, and the survivors of the eventual War in victorious joy on their stumps and tails, ready to rebuild with their flippers. Lately, the Menace has been put on the defensive, however, by the Americans advancing, the Soviets standing firm, and the survivors, etc. . . .

But the War may be too late, say the fans of Ecological Doom. Acid rain and a sudden ice age caused by aerosol destruction of the ozone layer will combine with nuclear waste spewing out of earthquake-torn dumps to make short shrift of us before anyone can push a button.

The outstanding feature of all the Impending Disaster theories seems to be their competitive spirit, their urge to get there before the others do. They are in a race with each other for the 1990s, and although they are all perfectly feasible and stand a healthy chance of making it, I now propose a new Disaster, guaranteed to overtake the others in the time it takes you to locate your Civil Defense shelter on the map you don't have.

My generation of post-war baby boom babies will be in the majority very shortly in the United States, if we aren't already. We have been marked by the singular experience of the 1960s in ways we did not have time to evaluate and understand before the brutal economics and political reaction of the 1970s overcame us like nitrous oxide.

What happened in the seventies was a wholesale scramble for places in the society previously spurned. All those old degrees, from institutions once thought malevolent, came back like the family silver that had been buried in the garden. People who had not finished school went back to it, as did some of the returning Vietnam veterans. (Curiously enough, the dropouts, who had been enemies of the war, and the veterans, who fought it, found themselves in the same position in the 1970s: Nobody wanted to talk about it, their experience was better off forgotten.)

The vast push for social reintegration demanded that all old experience be put aside in all its curious inconclusiveness until another day. Millions of peoples' old personalities were suddenly in storage, in deep freeze, out of sight, out of mind. As the new, status-conscious, conforming and performing personalities of young professionals took control of the place grudgingly vacated for them by the ever-upwardly-mobile (but for how long?) older Americans, a certain vacuum was beginning to be felt, a hollow sound at the core of the being.

Rip Van Winkle started to stir. Periodically, the electricity went out and the personality in deep freeze started to thaw. The energy crises, of fuel and of growing older, made people want to go deeper into the roots of what ailed them and their society. The fact that many of the sixties outsiders are now the majority of insiders on the middle management levels of the communication and marketing industries made the necessity for investigation even more urgent; for how can you communicate and sell something when you don't know either yourself or the people you're addressing?

It is clear now that something is about to break down, namely, the huge generational freezer system wherein lies the body of our outsider experience from the 1960s. The freezing process, which I named Psycho-Cryogenics, like its mortuary kin, must now be reversed if our society is to keep its balance. In my opinion, this is impossible without letting out of the bag more demons than we can handle.

But since the Huge Thaw is going to happen whether we like it or not, and has already begun, I predict that sixty percent of my generation, millions of American citizens, that is, are heading for Imminent Mental Breakdown. IMB can strike at any given moment, without warning, quicker than an earthquake, more shocking than acid rain, and certainly less calculated than either provincial autonomy or limited nuclear war.

The crack that runs through my generation threatens to make all these other disasters nonfunctional for the simple reason that nothing can go according to plan when madness has been suddenly introduced in the blueprint. Besides, what use for oil has a man who prefers to walk on his hands?

Coldwar Jollies

———

When Rocky's fist went through Ivan Drago's face, something in me saluted him. And when Baryshnikov, in sneakers and bluejeans, smoking a Marlboro cigarette, did some anti-KGB funk boogie to some black disco blasting from a big box, I nearly cried: Right ON! The Cold War is back, and it isn't a contest of ideas any more, if it ever was. It's between bluejeans and baggy suits, between jogging and being trained by a machine, between the lone cowboy and the faceless gang. It's a battle of styles, and ours are obviously better. Even the apolitical, classical language of ballet must give way. Misha dances on point in his sneakers, not in ballet slippers like dancers East and West used to. And he *smokes* while he dances! When the KGB man is being nice, he tries to keep up with the Joneses: he claims a sophisticated acquaintance with the West. But clearly, he's a pretender: deep down he's a brutal Russian *mujik,* who doesn't know his jeans from his burlap. Rocky's fist and Misha's jeans may be among the most durable fictions of our time. Yevgheni Yevtushenko, the Russian poet who only recently called for greater economic freedom in the Soviet Union, blasted the new Cold War movies as dreadful anti-Soviet propaganda. That may be, but once greater economic freedom puts the Russians in blue jeans, these movies may well be meaningless. Like opposing football teams on a black and white TV, it will be too hard to tell who's who if everyone's wearing the same thing. Ultimately, Hollywood may save the world. Only Hollywood can make the Cold War a matter of style. And only Hollywood has, in recent movies, destroyed more military hardware than most countries possess. Planes, tanks, submarines, jets, and missiles splatter the screens. Given enough clout Hollywood can disarm the world. Hand the Pentagon to the major studios, and put the Russians in bluejeans. The millenium's at hand.

Subs

————

The alleged Hitler diary and the submarine paranoia presently gripping Norway and Sweden, have something in common: they are both about deeply buried things. Hitler is an unsettling object in the muddy bottom of our Western psyche. The subs, which no depth charges seem capable of bringing up, are likewise troubling subterranean facts. Should Hitler's diaries be forged, which seems almost certain, it will mean only that he will not be so easily forced to light: The depth charge of this massive forgery will have failed. Should the subs turn out to be real, which is also likely, means only that the things lurking under us are indeed to be feared because they *are* real.

Hitler made submarine warfare what it is today. There was already, in that German effort to sneak silently undercover and kill suddenly, the clear sign of our century's tendency to bury everything bothersome out of sight. In the light of day, Germany marched, sang songs, and put on symbolic pageants. Underwater and at night, it murdered. Simon Wiesenthal, the Nazi-hunter, said that the alleged diaries may be "an attempt to clean up Hitler." I think it is only yet another attempt to find out what Hitler means, another attempt to make sense of the present time which is so much a consequence of Hitler's age. The market simply demands such forgeries.

Today, the world is held hostage by submarines. American and Soviet nuclear submarines silently patrol the oceans' bottoms, armed with enough atomic warheads to lay the planet waste. Underwater, out of mind, seems to be the unspoken assumption about those dark shapes floating in our unconscious. Occasionally, an American and a Soviet sub collide or nearly collide underwater: Their missiles roll silently into the ocean

mud, and nothing is said by either power. The watery grave
does not disturb the surface of our bright cheeriness.

Norway and Sweden, one occupied by Hitler, the other
neutral, are suddenly fearing the subs lurking under their waters.
But those aren't subs, even if they turn out to be: They are
Hitler's diaries, bottled in long, unsettling cylinders.

Digging It: Beware of the Hollow Sound

Word comes from England that the *Masquerade* treasure has been found, marking the end of a long search by thousands of treasure hunters. The clues had been contained in *Masquerade,* a book by the English artist Kit Williams, who buried a jeweled rabbit on August 8, 1979. The man who found it was quoted as saying: "When I found it, I felt right dejected. There was nothing to live for."

It was a publicity stunt all right, but it revealed something about human nature, namely, that we are eternal children. The gardening season is upon us, and I bet that at least half of us take up the shovel with the secret hope that we might uncover something hidden in the ground by somebody. Right under that skunk cabbage, there may be a pirate's treasure chest. With little to look forward to in the so-called "real" world, that skunk cabbage hole may be our best bet.

In California and Nevada, the price of gold has been sending people to the hills in droves looking for abandoned mines and panning sites. The gold is only a pretext. The real reason for all that digging is the hope of uncovering a secret. A man has been photographed next to a giant nugget saying: "I've known it all along. I had a dream about it."

Beachcombers with buzzing machines walk through throngs of bathers, aware only of the faint buzzing in their ear phones. In the cities, a whole population of stubborn seekers dives into garbage, looking for a lost diamond earring but content to find an old shirt. Other people, lost to their fellow pedestrians, walk with their eyes on the ground, looking for money. And the world over, children dig holes in the ground by any means they can, the deeper the better.

Unfortunately, we have been creating garbage at a rate that surpasses by far the abilities of even the best diggers among us. Whole portions of the earth have become off limits to our digging and dreaming. Who would go digging in a radioactive waste dump? Even the most idyllic spot on earth may not be entirely without danger, even if there are no signs advising us to stay away. Illegal dumping is big business.

But even if we aren't likely to stumble on a chemical dump, there is still the matter of all the underground architecture our governments have been preparing for us to live in, in the event of nuclear war. How much of the earth has been honeycombed with the mad plans of military fantasy is anybody's guess.

In the sixties, official "time capsules" were buried all over this country, containing what was called "the best accomplishments of our civilization." I have no idea what's in those "time capsules," but I can assure you that "the best" of anything isn't in there.

Most likely, the most boring of everything has been encapsulated, things like school books, bad translations of the classics, horrible recordings of stupid ceremonies, texts of ponderous political proclamations, and all sorts of symbolic trivia like flags, lapel pins, and commemorative stamps.

In *Planet of the Apes,* a science fantasy about the survivors of a nuclear holocaust, some of the characters find an intact atom bomb and build a religion around it. That is a lot more likely than stumbling on the complete recordings of Beethoven and worshiping those.

The problem with the saccharine imaginings of the people who would preserve our culture is the abominable ignorance of what truly constitutes present-day culture. The last time I looked around, the deadly, shiny new toys of the military had a far superior grace and physical beauty than the vinyl discs of RCA.

Today's art and culture reflect more than anything the horrendous fear of what those toys may be doing to us. Burying and encapsulating is a futile exercise: We are only burying what should be always open and kept in the light for as long as possible: the assertion of the individual voice against the collective machinations of the powers over us.

Meanwhile, we may go on dreaming. But beware of the hollow sound that tells you that your gardening spade may have hit a treasure chest. It may not be a treasure chest at all, but a shiny cylinder full of death.

Riddle of the Vessels

I have wondered for years about which lost vessel would be found first: Noah's Ark or the *Titanic*. It turned out to be the latter. We'll have to wait a while longer for the evidence of what Noah *really* took on the Ark with him. Meanwhile we'll have to make do with knowing what Charlotte Drake Martinez Cardeza took with her on the *Titanic*. Fourteen trunks of clothing and trinkets, and a bag of jewels by one account. One of these jewels, the Pink Diamond, was heavily insured and claims were duly lodged. Only some folks say that Charlotte took the jewels into the lifeboat with her.

None of Noah's animals was insured. The purpose of the Ark's voyage was, for that matter, quite different from that of the *Titanic*. The Ark went out to save life from perishing under the waters of the flood. The *Titanic* went out to save the rich from boredom on land. The Ark ended, presumably, on a mountain top. The *Titanic*, under the waters.

When we find Noah's Ark, we will have a part of the Bible come to life. With the *Titanic*, The Great Gatsby himself has surfaced. It is like pulling the glittering twenties from their watery grave. Not many decades sink as definitely as the twenties. The *Titanic* wasn't just a ship: it was the gilded age between the wars, compressed in a boat the way F. Scott Fitzgerald squeezed it into a book. The *Titanic* had to sink. It crashed like the market. A boat like this seems such a symbol that it's a little eerie to have the real thing all of a sudden. After so many songs, movies, and legends, we are surprised with the clumsiness of a real body. The real *Titanic* looks puny next to the legendary one. I say, let's forget it and go after Noah's Ark. And when we find that one, let's forget it and go after the Grail. Some things are better off legendary.

Dread

Dread isn't just another fear. Dread is that middle of the night grip on your soul that encompasses the universe. There is no fear that has the range and depth of dread. It's what Melville had in mind when he said: "Though in many of its aspects, this visible world seems formed in love, the invisible spheres were formed in fright."

You are never prepared to enter these invisible spheres. There was a time, when someone dear to me died, when I felt that a hole had opened in the familiar and I was about to be sucked through. The edges of the hole were made of fear. The center of it was sheer dread. A guy who'd been in the Vietnam War told me about a kind of fear he once felt in the jungle. "It was pure electric terror. Nothing civilians can tell you anything about."

There are grades of fear and shadings of terror. They span the ranges from apprehension to dread. We experience them seismically, like tremors of varying magnitudes. The earthquake in Mexico City filled me with dread. I have dear friends living there and to this date, when I am speaking this, I don't know if they are alright or not. The American Embassy has not heard from them. I don't want to think of the worst, but I can't help it. They lived in the hardest-hit area.

I inherit a penchant for dread from my mother. Fires, floods, earthquakes, and other cataclysms run through her dreams nightly. She used to imagine me consumed by flames or squashed by cars if I was a hour late. *There* is proof, if any is needed, that imagining it doesn't necessarily make it so. But dread is deeper than imagination. It is the voice of our deepest and no doubt repressed experiences. The race dies and dies. The voice of its suffering translates and echoes in every human being. Its language is dread. We speak to ourselves that way.

Treasure

My mother has had a dream of riches ever since she came to America. This is, of course, the standard immigrant dream. As my grandmother used to say: In America dogs walk around with pretzels on their tails.

My mother is a printer. She makes a decent living but is decidedly not rich. So she plays the lottery every day like millions of others and drops a buck or two on boxers and football games where she works, although she knows nothing about either boxing or football. Mother has an infinite belief in her luck, in *pure* luck, I should say, because she often wins football and boxing bets. Therefore, she concludes, winning has nothing to do with expertise.

So one fine morning last week I took her to Atlantic City, to the "big time." On the chartered bus everyone's spirit rode high, and my mother made conversation with a woman her age who told her that a neighbor of a neighbor of someone her sister knows had hit the jackpot on a slot machine and came home with a clear fortune. To this, my mother added that the sister of a cousin of a neighbor of a man she works with had done the same thing nary two weeks before. Maybe they are the same person, I thought; statistics are funny. But why spoil the fun?

Part of the charter deal was a free meal on arrival. Hundreds of other bus travelers from the East Coast made long animated lines in the restaurant. The cousin of the neighbor of the man was frequently mentioned. The food was terrific and there was plenty of it, but mother could barely eat. Here, within reach of treasure, food seemed out of place. The sumptous fruit salad, which anywhere else would have starred in my mother's conversation, was merely another impediment. But it was soon over and done with, so we headed for the heart of the magic cave.

The sweeping view of the casino from the top of the stairs was breathtaking. Red lights made an aura of mysterious gaudiness about the thousands of people swaying before whirring, dancing, jumping money machines. The spinning roulette wheels threw dizzying glimmers of hope to the ceilings where hidden men watched the action on TV. At the blackjack tables, ordinary K-Mart clothes took on sophisticated airs. My mother's image of a casino came, I am sure, from old movies, where pale and amorous men in dinner jackets move in hushed silence and old world splendor through the pits of the Riviera. Well, this was no Monte Carlo as she could plainly see. This was a big democratic country and nobody cared how you dressed as long as you had the chips.

I left mother with a big paper cup of quarters in front of a warm one-armed bandit and wished her good luck. I then wandered off to find my own destiny. It was a long time before I returned. My destiny, it turns out, had led me to a seat at a blackjack table just vacated by a loser. The ions were going the wrong way and I became their victim. Broke but stoic I then began to search for mother.

For a moment I panicked: I thought I had lost her. Looking over the identical rows of thousands of humming machines, each one with a middle-aged lady in a green polyester suit in front of it, I couldn't tell who she was.

It was a movement that gave her away: she pulled the lever of the machine with the extraordinary energy of which only she is capable and which enables her, even at the age of sixty, to do the work of several people at her job. She looked so determined I feared that she might pull the machine from its stem. Cherries whirled past, and apples, and out of the tumbling fruit mother came. Her cup was nearly empty, but not "until it's all gone," would she stop. The piercing shriek of a wounded animal rent the air purple, and yellow flashing lights announced to the world that not far from us the cousin of the sister of the neighbor of a man who knew someone we know had hit the jackpot.

When mother's cup was empty, we strolled on the boardwalk. It felt good to be broke and to know what we knew all along:

the only free pretzels in the world are on the tails of the dogs in my grandmother's dreams.

"Too bad," mother said, "I didn't eat the plums and cherries in the fruid salad. Those were real."

Maybe so.

Exxon

The other day I woke up in the Soviet Union. It doesn't happen very often, but there it was. The tall forties-style building that could have been the I. V. Stalin Typographical Union. The statue of Molotov with the adoring masses crawling up his sides. The industrial haze that turned everything the color of lead.

When I came to my senses, I realized that, of course, the Huey Long Capitol Building in Baton Rouge is not the I. V. Stalin building, although they are both masterpieces of Social Realism. Nor is the statue over Huey Long's grave a statue of Molotov, although their pose looks strikingly similar.

The above is only a small part of something that's been happening to me lately, something truly peculiar. I experience a kind of geographical, political, and spiritual superimposition between the United States and the Soviet Union. The large bureaucratic institution where I work is ruled by petty gossip, innuendo, and rumor just like any Moscow counterpart. Writing, which is my métier, seems to be turning, more and more, into a system of government and academic rewards and punishments that has nothing to do with the writing itself. There are writers' colonies everywhere, for instance, just like there are in the USSR. And the people who go there go because their writing is safe and inoffensive.

Elsewhere in American life, there are also signs of a Soviet-like malaise. Air-pollution and the environment take a back seat to industry in both countries. Nuclear stockpiling goes unchecked.

The same morning that I had my social realist vision I smelled perfume in the air. Since it was not the season, and it was smoggy as usual outside, I wondered what it could be. Then I had the sudden intuition that Exxon had been perfuming the smog.

A pleasantly toxic confusion seems to be enveloping the planet.

Poison

This is the age of poison. Within days of the Tylenol-cyanide scandal, a wave of domestic product poisonings swept the country. A couple in Iowa was arrested in a plot to taint milk with insecticide. Visine eyedrops laced with acid were found in Florida. In Ohio there was strychnine-tainted milk. Acid-spiked Lavoris was also found in Florida.

Horror is not true horror until it is lodged in the familiar. All these mad attacks are aiming for the little core of security at the very heart of the family: the medicine cabinet, the morning glass of milk. Family life in America, as pictured in advertising, consists of a series of untroubled rituals which, if used regularly, will act as exorcisms against the troubles of the world. If you brush your teeth, the bad taste of things will go away. A few eyedrops should relieve tiredness and drudgery. Headache, which is another trace of the real world, should disappear when you take aspirin. And milk, in all its literal and metaphorical meanings, represents the very essence of security. It represents mother and children and country. It is no coincidence that there were two unrelated attacks on it within days of each other. What all these attacks have in common is a mad desire to destroy the myth of ourselves as portrayed on television.

We live in an age of ecological awareness. Prophecies of environmental disaster are commonplace. Environmental disasters are commonplace. Every day the government and the universities issue new warnings concerning the stuff we eat, drink, wear, or smoke. The number of warnings has increased geometrically in the past few years. Someone with a detailed memory for such things would have to live in a world of fear. Everything is poisoned or potentially poisoned. Our ability to function depends on ignoring the truth about the environment. But there is only so much that can be ignored before it gets worse. As a culture, we've made our bed and now we must lie in it.

Seen in perspective then, those individual acts of sabotage are only personalized versions of the ways we attack ourselves collectively. In an era when public villains are chemicals, it is no surprise that nostalgic criminals would want a piece of the action. People used to clamor to join criminal gangs. Now they want to join the evils going by the names Lead, Acid, Strychnine. There is a doomsday bandwagon rolling by and all sorts of unhappy people want to get on it.

There was a popular plot idea in the 1960s, often mentioned as a joke by hippies, about putting LSD in the water supplies of major cities. The people who mentioned it usually looked favorably on the results because they believed in LSD. The anarchy resulting from such an action would have to be beneficial, they argued, because LSD strips away peoples' defenses. By becoming vulnerable, people would somehow also become better. The idea was a contemporary of the war in Vietnam and was, in some way, a protest.

The Vietnam War was an ecological nightmare whose consequences we are still suffering. The defoliation of the Vietnamese jungles with Agent Orange did not stop there. Chemical and bacteriological warfare, banned by many existing treaties, has been developed, tested, and used intensively since the 1960s. In Afghanistan, the Soviets reportedly have been using bacteriological weapons. Germ warfare was also reported in Cambodia. With mass-murder chemical and biological weapons in place, we ought to feel pretty well settled at the heart of a global nightmare. The military and corporate nature of these poison systems has depersonalized death, however, leaving crazy romantics no recourse but to cut themselves a piece of cake with their name on it.

It used to be considered bad form to be paranoid. Well, no more. So much that seemed to be a matter of fantasy or horror fiction has come to pass that being paranoid may, in fact, be the only way to stay sane.

The crazy poisoners are alerting us to the obvious. What is the difference between industry-tainted PCB milk in Michigan and personally-tainted insecticide milk in Iowa? One is impersonal, incalculably devastating, and seemingly unconscious. The other is criminal, clumsy, and supposedly intentional. But the last is only a miniaturized mirroring of the first.

Two Kinds of Law

There are many people now taking industry to court for giving them cancer. It is extremely hard to prove. Certain kinds of cancer have been traced directly to certain kinds of pollution. Vinyl chloride and liver cancer, for instance. Even so, the burden of proof rests on the plaintiff, and there are thousands of variables.

The time has come, I think, to have two kinds of law. One for people, and another for technology and industry. It is all very well and noble to presume people innocent until proven guilty. That's a great statement of faith in human beings. But can we assume the same about machines?

Do we even have the same aims? What if the aim of technology is simply to perpetuate itself, regardless and in spite of human beings? Can we expect machines to have our interests at heart? Of course not. Why should they?

The history of technological progress since the Industrial Revolution is not reassuring. While machines have come to occupy center stage in the world, human beings are becoming quickly marginalized. We can barely move without our mechanical devices, our memories have been replaced by information stored outside of ourselves, our leisure time has been invaded by electronic programming. All those qualities by which we used to know the human animal are being slowly usurped as machine-made mimetic ones replace them.

Clearly, at some unknown point in time, humans and their tools have parted company. As for what that *means* you have only to look at the rising cancer rates on the one hand, and our spiritual malaise on the other.

Let's debunk the insidious cliché that machines serve us, or that they are only as good as the people running them. Most people know only how to push buttons. Unlike people, industry should be presumed guilty until found innocent. We can't afford to extend our humanity to what may very well be our enemy.

PCBs

———

I was warned to expect strange people in my yard because I live near the State Capitol. People bring their grievances here. But I did not expect ten thousand of them, when I came home from work the other day. I saw them from a way off as I walked across the park. They were carrying large signs and swaying. I heard them also, making an odd and eerie sound.

As I got closer, the signs came into view. ABORTION IS MURDER. HITLER WOULD'VE LOVED IT. JESUS LOVES EVERY-BODY.

Well, I wasn't so sure about that as I tried to cross the human wave to get to my house. For one thing, everybody had closed ranks so tightly and was singing so hard I doubt that anything short of a cannon would have made them budge for someone *going the other way*. They all seemed to be nice, conservatively dressed folk, but there was definitely something glazed, auto-matic, and weird about them.

As I made my way to the middle of the parade, the vortex of sound almost sucked me up. S-W-E-E-T JEEEEZZUS. SWEET JEEEEZZZUS. I almost rose to heaven right on the spot. I almost started maching too. The hypnotic procession gave me the goosebumps like a medieval crusade would. It was the twelfth century and it worked.

While this was going on, the Rollins Corporation across the river quietly announced plans to burn an unbelievable quantity of PCBs in the atmosphere. As my birthday present, I suppose.

So much PCB, most scientists agree, is enough to cause cancers to grow visibly as you breathe. Add those to the fact that we now hold the nation's numero uno spot for liver and pancreas cancers, and you can say without exaggerating that we live in hell.

But are the good Christians in my front yard interested in hell? Hell, no, they don't mind living in it. The only thing they mind is other people's business.

Monsters

Recently, in China, a team of scientists discovered one hundred legendary lake monsters in Hanas Lake near the border between Mongolia and China. The monsters are red, weigh one ton, and are a variety of salmon.

At the same time, in Alloy, West Virginia, a chemical company town, things have been undergoing monstrous transformations. Chevrolets began melting on the street, peoples' shoes oozed into the sidewalk as they were walking, and the forearm of Saint Anthony, holding a book in front of the local church, fell off the torso. Union Carbide, whose chemicals appear to be responsible for the various metamorphoses of things in Alloy, West Virginia, responded by staging parades with the theme: WE LOVE CARBIDE.

There is a link between the Chinese monsters in Outer Mongolia and the melted Chevrolets in West Virginia. They are all manifestations of the extraordinary, which is beginning to intrude upon our lives more and more. The harder we try to deny the existence of the monstrous, the more it surfaces. In the Chinese case, the monsters stayed shrouded in legend for thousands of years, only to surface suddenly into fact. In West Virginia, the monstrous was disguised as the everyday reality of work and wages, until it suddenly bust through the outlines of things and changed them. The end of legends is something we seem to wish, even as we create new ones. The end of the Chinese legend may be the end of the monsters it once hid. The Union Carbide legend—namely, that it makes useful things like everybody else, while keeping the folks in Wonderbread—is also nearing the end. There is a difference, too, between the uncovering of the monstrous and the production of it. Let's hope that when the legend bursts the monsters go with it.

Ceremonies of the New Right; or, The Peoples' Religion

I went to the grand opening of Jimmy Swaggart's World Ministries on Easter—to mingle with the folk. After the opening hymns, Brother Swaggart took after Communism. The day they laid Jesus in the grave, he said, was humanity's darkest day. It was Friday. Yeah, but Sunday came! And right now in Poland they are celebrating Easter under the Russian jackboot! It's Friday in Poland! But Sunday is coming! And in Afghanistan the Russian soldiers are killing villages-full of innocent women and children! It's Friday in Afghanistan! But Sunday is coming!

The 7,000 faithful, who were neither too well heeled nor too handsome, turned up their palms to receive the spirit from brother Jimmy's hand-held microphone. Just above the stage, a most professional mixing board had skillful hands laid upon it. And the TV cameras blazed away. After which Brother Swaggart took after the media, prancing all over the stage at least half as good as his cousins Jerry Lee Lewis and Mickey Gilley, with whom he is co-emperor of the lower middle-class. The media, he said, doesn't know the Gospels. They think it's a waste for us to spend 120 million dollars on television . . . a waste to spread the word of the Lord . . . meanwhile that "demon-possessed freak Prince" made $116 million last year!

I had the distinct feeling here that a revelation was about to break forth from the preacher's lips, and sure enough it came: Jesus said I'm here to take away the sin of the world, and the other day—said Brother Jimmy—I was in the TV studio and the man in the booth said to Me: "Take it all away, Jimmy!"

Now that's talent, and the faithful recognized it and were gripped by the spirit. And later they called out from a sheet that had been passed among them: "Help us Jesus to preserve our Judeo-Christian tradition from the menace of secular humanism!"

A few snagged their tongues on those hard last words. But what matter a few slips of the tongue to those speaking in tongues?

How Right You Are

At a time when Left and Right are once again assuming a sharp ideological edge, it is useful to remember that these notions mean little today.

Vasily Axyonov, an émigré Soviet writer, describes himself as part of the Soviet Left. He then pauses to explain that Left and Right in the USSR don't mean the same as they do here. The Stalinists are Right and the liberals, like himself, are Left. But in the United States he finds, to his dismay, that the Left doesn't like him, while the Right applauds. Perhaps the only way to keep things straight, he says, is to do what recruits in Peter the Great's army used to do: keep a few bits of straw under the left shoulder of your tunic to tell you exactly where left is. When ordered to march, Peter's soldiers were bid to proceed, Hay! Right! Hay! Right!

I personally can't tell left from right unless I listen to my heart. I attribute this to a case of organic anarchism. The truth is that most of us live in a state of ideologically-induced guilt and contradiction: We eat meat that's bad for us, we drive polluting cars and pay taxes for the killing machine. The Guilty Liberal condition is now the generalized state of affairs. Left and Right under these circumstances represent not political realities but emotional states: Left can be loosely assigned to the ideal of "how things should be," and Right to "how things are." In *Realpolitik* these days, the People belong to the Right, and populism is the Right philosophy. All things that can be easily explained, that have the crystalline charm of self-evident utterance are the property of the Right. The Left inherits the complexity of details, the frightening figures, the economic dryness, the environmental nightmare, the nuclear horror. But language isn't with it. The Right has all the language that "makes sense." The Left has clumsy facts on one hand, clichés on the other. Wed the boredom of fact to the weariness of cliché and what do you have? A morality without language, an ideology in mothballs. As language, the *esprit du temps* shows the rightness of Rightism, the gaucheness of Leftism.

In literature the old directions have long ago lost all meaning. To speak of Left and Right in letters is to evidence the naiveté of the Old Left. The urge for ideological definition, for a taking of "stands on issues," reflects only a desire to transcend the current critical approaches to art. Or the lack of them. The desire for critics is itself a desire for a return to order, a sign of the times: an Old Leftist sentiment with a Rightist modus operandi.

Even in the Third World, the circumspect use of ideological direction reflects convenience rather than faith, cynical sloganeering as opposed to romanticism.

It seemed almost clear for a while there, in the late sixties and early seventies that a new, nonideological, humanist solution might be the answer to relentless rhetorical polarization. But we are far from that now, as we are being quickly returned to a black and white view of the world.

Melanoia

I discovered a new disease called "melanoia" in a book called *Mordecai of Monterey* by Keith Abbott. It's a California disease, but with a little luck it can spread all over the country. Medically, melanoia is the opposite of paranoia. Wherever Mordecai, the book's hero, goes, he is haunted by the feeling of something good happening to him. When he hears a PING! in his head, he begins to follow someone; and then this someone brings him unbelievable luck, sometimes in downright cold cash.

In California, of course, some people still operate under a set of social-cosmic intercourse rules called "vibes." Vibes have, for the most part, disappeared from most of the rest of the country. They have been replaced by the dry facts. Where not so long ago one could go on vibes as far as another person was concerned, now nothing will be done without a look at the files. Questions like: What do you do for a living? Have you lived here long? Are you originally from here? have all replaced the Vibe Age questions: What's your sign? Have you read Siddhartha? and What are the vibes like around here? The new questions are paranoic. The old ones were melanoic. The paranoic questions aim to get at the bottom line, which is social acceptability. They are exclusionary. The melanoic questions are adventure-seeking. They open up in the unpredictable. The unpredictable, of course, can sometimes be an unpleasant experience. But it can also take you places the new predictability can't conceive of.

I was so pleasantly—and why not, nostalgically—struck by Mordecai's melanoia, I wished to immediately catch it. Alas, it's only symptomatic of our times that adventurousness and unpredictability have to be introduced as some kind of disease. A disease is about as factual as you can get. It's not like vibes, which are vague, and in the way. A disease you can trust: it's got a solid data base.

So how's the old melanoia, eh?

Our Cyphered Dystopia

A new map of the world is in the offing, a map both truer and finer than the official one. A number of imaginary countries have been appearing in literature. Some of these are real countries that have ceased to exist. Others are countries where history has been so patently falsified that only the most monumental and radical rewriting could restore them. Others yet have never existed, but their mythic descriptions have the impact of reality.

The authors of these countries are mostly Eastern Europeans and Latin Americans, people on the periphery of the Western world but clearly at the center of Western consciousness. Conspicuously missing from this map, which is as yet largely blank, like a medieval map, are the imaginings of North Americans and Western Europeans. The countries at the center of the West are, paradoxically, on its creative periphery.

Central Eastern Europeans and Latin Americans work, of course, from different premises and are under different exigencies to create. For all that, we are no less in need of a creative rethinking of our world. The French imagination has been retreating in language. Americans are confined by a painful neorealism, consisting of relentless descriptions of trivia.

Of those countries that have ceased to exist, Czeslaw Milosz's Lithuania is one of the most complete. The awesome responsibility of being at once the preserver and the author of his country makes Milosz a kin of the earliest chroniclers of history. The scribes of the beginning and the exiled poet of the end make two parentheses trying to contain the mindless eraser of history.

A country named Masuria exists today only in a novel by Siegfried Lenz. I. B. Singer's Poland is a world like Chagal's: suspended just above the one that has taken its place.

In other places, where history has been rewritten, writers have become a combination of Atlas and Don Quixote, taking on impossible burdens. Solzhenitsyn is one of these tragic giants who almost singlehandedly has taken it upon himself to chronicle the underside of Russian history.

Latin American writers face a different challenge. Their history is schizophrenic, sharply divided between a fragmentary memory of the Indian past and a postcolonial world still in the process of definition. For them the circular workings of magical time continue invisibly within the linearity of our Western notions of progress.

Carlos Fuentes's *Terra Nostra* and Gabriel Marquez's Macondo have taken their place in our consciousness with a kind of finality that the unstable map-marked countries of the region have yet to attain.

Surrounded by this demiurgy, American writers seem either unwilling or incapable of serious acts of imagination. We seem to be floundering in a sea of facts, a sort of cyphered dystopia that is, at best, a paranoid paradise. Most of the time, however, it manages to mean nothing. It is the very openness of American society, with its unending flood of information, that makes the creative gesture urgent. 25,000 credit cards, a 300,000-square foot building, 12 percent, and 20 miles NE, can coexist peacefully in the same newspaper paragraph, but we need more to understand.

Superficially, our craze for figures is not so different from the Soviet mania for letters. As Abram Terz tells us, there was a time in the USSR when: "All those acronyms like VTsik, TSik, RABKRIN, GUBISPOKOLM, NAROBRAZ, independently of the will of their creators, exuded some kind of lethal miasma, especially at night."

On their own, letters and numbers take on an ominous life. We can't allow them to take the place of thoughts in a new order of literacy where it is sufficient to know one's zip code.

The map is waiting.

Erasing the Past

An unprecedented project is taking place right now in
Bucharest, Romania. Nicolae Ceausescu, the dictator, is ordering the destruction of his historical captial to make room for
extravagant new monuments to himself. Nearly a quarter of this
great European city has fallen to his mania. The buildings
destroyed include sixteenth-century churches.

Ceausescu is viewed indulgently in the West as some kind of
maverick rebel in the Soviet camp. The reality of his country is
quite different. Now that Enver Hodja of Albania has joined
Stalin in the great Dictatorium in the Sky, Ceausescu has
assumed the number one Personality Cult in the world. In a
country that can ill afford it, monuments to the little, pudgy
man may well hide the long lines of miserable people waiting
before dawn for food. The singing of hosannas to him and his
family has been made mandatory. An all-pervasive secret police
apparatus, backed by an immense army of informers, makes sure
that the facade stays in place. Recent assassination attempts by
the Romanian secret police against dissident writers abroad have
brought him a great deal of negative publicity in Western
Europe. But in America we still think fondly of Ceausescu as the
man who facilitated the rapprochement between Nixon and
Mao, while giving us Nadia Comanici to demonstrate just how
it's done. Consequently, Romania has most-favored nation status and a great gymnastic reputation.

This latest caper, however, should not go unnoticed. Destroy-
ing history so that it might begin with him is too demented an
idea to let it pass. The last to try this was Albert Speer, Hitler's
architect, who wanted to "build buildings that would look good

in ruins" a thousand years hence. The thousand-year-old Reich lasted five years. And the ruins didn't look very good. Likewise in China, a mad emperor decreed that all the books be burned, that a Great Wall be erected, and that History should begin with Year One of His Reign. All these perverse efforts carried an eventually great, but more immediately, bitter lesson.

Make New

Looking at John White's drawings of America in 1585 (University of North Carolina Press) I am struck by the artist's fierce joy in the newness and strangeness of the New World. Animals, plants, landscapes, people, all are depicted with the enthusiasm of a child discovering a treasure.

It occurs to me that America's job ever since those days has been to produce newness and strangeness, in ever-increasing quantity. This we have done, at a staggering rate. When the newness of natural things appeared to wear off, or was adopted by the old world, America produced a seemingly endless stream of technical innovations. The rest of the world took it for granted that our product was inexhaustible.

When American technical innovations were also adopted everywhere, the world looked to us for psychological innovation. This, too, we dutifully contributed in the decades just past, with our mass enthusiasms for various new models of human behavior.

But somewhere along the way things began to change. America's childhood, full of the wonders of John White's drawings, gave way to America's brilliant innovative adolescence, which in its turn is giving way to a reluctant middle-age.

The desire for the new and the strange has been yielding to a new conformism, a lack of curiosity with the world, and an obsessive preoccupation with ourselves. The young today seem prematurely old. My own students are older than me in the one respect that matters: the future.

To my generation, the future was an adventure. To them it's a search for security. I pity the poor emigrant, as the song says, arriving in the xenophobic, uptight, careerist middle-age of today's America.

I was lucky to come when I did. I was new right before the world got old.

The Heavy Door

A European friend visiting America shared her impressions with me this way:

"At first," she said, "I was overwhelmed by the vastness of it all. There is so much room and so much beauty here. I went to a little town on the eastern shore of Maryland and couldn't believe that a landscape like that, with the little church, and the river and the wooded hills, was not completely full of vacationers, picnickers, and tourists. A place like that, in Europe, would attract thousands every day. I went back there several times but I began to feel anxious. There was something lacking, something I couldn't put my finger on. My exhilaration gave way to a kind of apprehension. At the same time, I was reading the American papers and watching TV, and I was beginning to feel that a heavy information door had clanged shut behind me. There was suddenly no real news of the rest of the world, only condescending little items. All there was was America. A beauty queen who took her clothes off dominated the news for a week at the same time that several wars raged in the world, unmentioned and unnoticed. There seems to be a relation here between the anxious beauty and vastness of this country and its self-obsession and isolation."

My European friend went on like this, and for a few moments I saw us through her eyes, the way I had also seen once. Indeed, what is a European to make of this immensity? For all our talk of overcrowding, our cities look like tiny dots of light on a huge body of wilderness. There is enough room here for millions of others. But we don't really want them here.

So we try to make believe that they do not exist.

Conceptual Namesake

I was working on my favorite pastime, trying to figure out what exactly is real these days, when a phone call came. The question of what is real didn't take much of my time until recently because I used to think that I had an instinct for it. But then, so does Coca Cola.

The phone call was from Willem de Ridder, a Dutch artist, who was calling between planes from New York to ask me if I wanted to go with him to a little Louisiana town called De Ridder—his namesake. Why not? I said.

De Ridder showed up dressed in a flowing cape with a silk bow tie. He was also lugging state-of-the-art recording and camera equipment with a view to capturing every precious moment of his purely linguistic disembarking. Purely linguistic because the town had been named from Amsterdam by a Dutch merchant who owned property along the railroad but never set foot in America. Because he was a foreigner and I don't drive, we took the Trailways bus and were soon on our way toward a tiny dot on the map near the Texas border.

It was a cold and miserable day. The bus lurched forward in the rain through the rural South, making brief stops in tiny towns along the way. Poverty the likes of which has been well hidden in most of the country, came in. People with cardboard suitcases tied with string, soldiers on leave still wearing their uniforms, families lugging huge trunks with all their belongings.

While De Ridder was voice-testing his equipment in Dutch, a clump of Mexican farmworkers climbed aboard the bus—on their way, no doubt, to a sugarcane plantation. At that moment, a brand new Eldorado pulled into the puddle of the bus station.

The migrants all rose from their seats pointing excitedly out the window. In their minds, they were already driving it.

The town of De Ridder was all closed gas stations and church neon. Not only that, but it was dry. You had to go to Texas for a drink. "Hey, you the new preacher?" shouted a bunch of snotnosed kids from a porch. De Ridder took a lot of pictures. The city dumpster, the abandoned gas station, the closed drug-store.

I figured out what's real. The bus. The bus is real.

Two Americas

There are two Americas: there is the America that drives, and
there is the America that takes the bus. If you watch television,
the only America you see is the America that drives. The
America that drives lives on the other side of the TV sceen from
the America that takes the bus. There used to be a time when
the America that takes the bus was heard from, be it ever so
little. There was a time when the poor rode the bus to the other
side of the TV screen to surprise the middle class as they
lounged about the modular living room. There was a time when
the poor would hitchhike into the consciousness of middle-class
America through the books of certain writers. The disen-
franchised, the wretched, and the poor could always hitch a ride
through one of Jack Kerouac's lines of prose, straight into the
inner sanctums of TV land. But in this age of Reagan, the TV
glass has become hard and impenetrable. To take the bus now is
to be surprised by the sheer madness and anger out there. It isn't
just the "normal" poor folk, if there is such a thing, going
Greyhound these days. Crazies of all stripes ride too. There are
drugged crazies, certified lunatics discharged by mental institutions, ex-cons going somewhere with one-way tickets. I can tell
the desperadoes on sight and try to avoid sitting next to them.
One guy told me he killed more people than there were on the
bus. Where? I asked him. Everywhere, he said, but mostly in
Vietnam. Another guy told me that he'd left a Bible in a motel
in Hollywood and now they are making a movie from the parts
he underlined. Another showed me a pistol and told me the
story of his tattoos. These people, I thought, are all clamoring
for their moment in the sun. They want the world to take
notice—but their desperate bullets ricochet off America's hard

TV screen. Even if they went off and killed some people, and some of them surely do, it will gain them no more than a few meager Andy Warhol moments in the fifteen-minute future. I only hope that the movie they are making from the underlined Bible has something in it about the man who underlined it. Hell's gonna break loose if it doesn't.

Chicken

Very softly, the old man murmured, "I'm sorry." He looked apologetically to the cashier, then to me, and then he met his wife's eyes. She nodded imperceptibly. As if brushing a leaf from his mohair coat which had seen better days, he removed the chicken from the pile of groceries on the counter. This chicken had formed the solid core of an otherwise meager store of provisions: instant french fries, one can of cut green beans, three of tomato sauce (small ones), a loaf of foamy bread, and a box of store brand spaghetti. Only a head of lettuce rivaled the chicken in size though not in importance.

"Is it enough?" the old man asked. The cashier made a rapid calculation. "Still eighty cents short," she said. Again, the apologies in two directions and the almost invisible look . . . With a gesture made gentler by the expectant silence, the old man pushed aside the lettuce. "Now," said the employee kindly, "You're only twenty-nine cents away." I reached instantly for my pocket and extracted the change, cursing myself for not having done it before, when the lettuce still remained. The man had difficulty accepting the change. But he did. "How can I ever repay you?" he said, sincerely.

About a week after this incident, I saw that chicken again. This time, it slipped into the large—though not seemingly so—pocket of a kindly grandmother bent over the chicken section as if studying the forms enveloped in plastic with an eye to some difficult menu. There must be secrets of sewing, accumulated in lifetimes of practice, which baffle safe crackers. When she straightened up, as I stood wondering how that big chicken had slipped so easily into such a narrow slit, she met my eye. A shot of panic went through her, but it disappeared instantly. In its stead was the defiant gaze of a tough. "Go ahead and tell on me," it said, "I've lived long enough." My eye hastened to reassure her. She wasn't grateful. She merely strode away to frown at the carrots. I saw her, on the way out, holding her bunch of California carrots like roses for a birthday.

The same chicken, dismembered and ready to enter the myriad recipes of the poor, haunts my childhood. Bent over the bird which had attracted her skillful eye, my grandmother pondered prices in the open air market behind the old Prefecture in my native town. This was in Eastern Europe, many years ago. She poked the legs to make sure they had as much meat on them as they appeared to. Lifted their wings to see if there was any fat under there. Throughout this inspection the chicken made an awesome racket. Even though its legs were tied together, its head and wings gyrated and beat furiously and the short beak took convulsive breaths.

For four years—and I was nearly four years and three months old at that moment—I had eaten nothing but chicken and apples. The chicken had come boiled, fried, sauteed, stuffed from my grandmother's hands, as surely and regularly as the clock's hands in the tower above the market. When we arrived home with the day's bird, I brought grandma the axe. She pinned the head down to the deeply criss-crossed stump and lowered it at once. I ran after the head while the body moved crazily all over the yard spurting blood. Bad as this scene was, I much prefer it to the endlessly quiet and perfectly dead plastic-wrapped bodies in today's supermarkets. My grandmother would have had nothing but contempt for these listless, identical animals grown like vegetables in huge factories. A chicken had, in those days, the benefit of having lived free, no matter how briefly. It had pecked at the corn, the gravel and the paint. It had judged, criticized, and yakked with other chickens. The freer it had lived (not the longer, though) the better it tasted. The highest compliment to any one of the thousands of chickens that contributed to our being, was to say "This one must have lived on the roof!" it being understood that the higher a chicken nested and the closer to the sun, the better it was.

When Louis XIV promised his peasants a chicken in every pot, he was describing an ideal future. Imagine what a chicken must have tasted like in Louis's time! It wasn't just what the chicken did, as in my grandmother's time, but also how rare it was. A free, unavailable chicken haunts the centuries! Today, the plastic package we push on that desultory moving rubber at the supermarket has as little in common with the *possible chicken* of Louis's France as filet mignon has to a hunted boar. Today's chicken is only a limp vegetable, drained of blood, full of chemicals, and tasteless.

Suddenly, I understood the deep gratitude of the old man, short twenty-nine cents. And the defiance of the old thief. Even if they had been poor all their lives, which I don't think was the case, it simply did not matter to them if they ate that chicken. Paid for or stolen, it made no difference. They had known the taste of chicken in times past, and what they were buying now could not come close to the aroma in memory. The man's deep gratitude had been only partly for my kindness. The other part had been reserved to the relief he felt at not having to ingest this synthetic product again. And the old thief's defiance had, likewise, been a challenge to me to denounce her, so that she could have the chickens she stole taken from her once and for all.

We underestimate old people when we concentrate solely on their poverty, which is both tragic and real. To those bleak aspects there comes another, as elusive as memory, as un-describable as taste or smell. This is the continual devaluation of basic pleasures in our world, food at the head of them, an inexorable, downward procession. The language we speak in the news as well as in public only compounds the confusion. Chicken today is not the same chicken as yesterday, or years ago.

Neither is money, of course. And we, are we to keep calling ourselves human beings, as we line up obediently at supermarket computers capable of picking our pockets as well as paralyzing shoplifters, and walk to our cars listlessly?

No, I think not. We should call ourselves chicken. We should rename everything else, too.

Beyond Gouda

It's cheaper to be rich. Being poor is terribly expensive. Take shopping, for instance. When I'm rich (very rarely and not lately) I shop like a butterfly or a nightingale. I pick an orange here, testing for smell, ripeness, and shimmer. I poke dreamily at a piece of cheese, to see if it's aged just right. I select my string beans, string bean by string bean, each one more perfectly stringless than the other. When I'm rich I can afford to travel a mile or two in search of a single loaf of French bread, and I will not shrink from leaving the country for a day if the perfect coffee should appear in a little shop beyond the border. And for all that, it is going to cost me less than shopping in penury.

When I'm broke, I shop for doomsday. First, I make sure that there are triples of every essential post-apocalypse food: flour, sugar, oil, spaghetti, tomato sauce, dead chickens, large size ground beef, enough rice to feed one hundred Cambodian refugees for one year, a small mountain of potatoes, and a tin mine's worth of cans filled with the cheapest California illegal alien produce.

The shopping carts of the poor are staggering objects, looking a bit like refugee wagons fleeing war and famine. Everything is balanced precariously because it has been thrown together in a hurry. Teetering on the edge of cans, glass bottles filled with brine and juice clank wildly under a top layer of toilet paper and the jumbo size generic paper towels.

You can tell the rich from the poor by the time they spend, too. The rich linger over the food and then take the fast lane. The poor wait, barely visible behind their mountains of basic hope, in long lines.

At home, too, the poor and the rich are vastly different

people. After selecting his orange and his slice of cheese, the well-heeled man either hands it to his cook or puts it on the counter until it is the perfect consistency to eat. He then turns on the stereo and reads a long list of boring figures by the light of the fireplace.

Not so the flat and busted. First, there is the problem of disposing of all the supplies so that they are close by at all times. The dead animals are quickly crammed into the freezer to lord it over the carrots and potatoes below. Everything else forms little hills and craggy surfaces around the house. The after-shopping geography of a poor person completely changes his living environment. Mountains of rice rise from previously smooth linoleum. Bouldery autumnal forests of onions have appeared near the sink. Pyramids of cans glare ritually from the corners, demanding human sacrifices. (They will have them soon, when the pauper cuts himself trying to open them.) In short, the poor's homes are arranged in such a way that they are entirely edible. From the bed or the living room sofa there can be no more than a short arm reach to the nearest starch.

The rich take their time eating. They savor the flavor, maybe with one eye closed, while listening to dinner music performed by white-jacketed musicians discreetly hidden behind a velvet curtain. After they have eaten, they drink strong, delicious coffee and read a long list of boring figures once again.

Next door, the poor are stuffing themselves. It is not enough that the food has been brought home. The anxiety of poverty tells them that it is still too far to the food, that an arm's length is an infinite distance for a person with arthritis, stroke, blindness, amputations, and paralysis. They must take this food inside their bodies as quickly as possible before any of those dread diseases strike. They gulp down mountains of rice, hills of potatoes, rivers of gravy. Now, that's better. After dinner, they drop right where they had been eating and fall into the soundless sleep of cholesterol.

The rich are skinny, the poor are fat. Only a hundred years ago it was the other way around. The glut of diet books on the best-seller lists testifies that the American dream is still alive. They are telling us that millions of people out there used to be fat (poor) and are now trying to become skinny (rich). The number of them who succeed are the measure of how the American Dream is faring these days. Not that well, I dare say, since they keep coming out with newer and better diets after people die trying to squeeze lemons on lettuce leaves.

Class

———

A student confided in me the other day. "You know," he said, "all teachers are commies." "No," I said, "I didn't know that." But I could just see that sprayed as graffiti all over the campus walls.

And what exactly are the students then? What exactly are these ruddy-cheeked, strapping healthy creatures that stroll vigorously across the lawns with their Reagan-Bush buttons? Are they not the advance guard of something as exotic as Commies? I must confess that I am not yet used to the sight of so many serene young Republicans. They believe in mom, apple pie and the flag with all the zeal of army commercials. God is on their side, and he is preppy, athletic, and carnivorous. They even sit in my poetry class, for Chrissakes. Poetry used to be the last refuge for uneasy liberals. Even art isn't safe, it seems, from their blue-eyed wonder. I must confess to a certain queasiness in the presence of excessive health and vitamins, especially when untroubled by thought. Just how deep and wide their innocence is can be gauged by the shocked disbelief they evince when I tell them, for instance, that Ronald Reagan ordered troops on campuses in California to teargas students. Nor have many of them heard of Hitler youth, likewise an overconfident young group from the days of yore.

Some of my colleagues have taken to calling their charges "Know-nothings," and the know-nothing jokes are sweeping the faculty lounges. "How many know-nothings does it take to screw in a lightbulb, etc. . . ."

The other day, a teacher was ordered to remove a male nude from a faculty art show. In the old days, he could have had the campus roaring. Instead, he meekly withdrew the work. That's the other side of so much overconfidence and moral self-righteousness, I told my friend. It makes cowards out of honest people.

It causes me to hear the faint marching of boots.

Americans at Last

Rick Barton, a local teacher, has had enough of low pay. Unlike most Americans enjoying the spoils of capitalism, teachers are paid by the state. They are regulated, preached at, held up to ridicule, and expected both to teach and to uphold moral principles so lofty no one in the real world has ever heard of them. In addition, they are regularly threatened with cuts, cutbacks, and rollbacks to keep them in line.

Rick has a solution now. It may do the trick of putting the last white-collar workers in America into that Yuppie heaven where there is always sailing weather. What Rick has in mind is simple and very American.

Every twenty minutes or so during his or her lecture, the teacher should pause and say, "The paper I have used to write my notes on has been made by Xerox." In another twenty minutes, he could hold up his pen and say, "It's a Bic. It has never failed me."

There are few captive audiences like those found in classrooms. There is a gold mine for advertisers there, and the teachers can pick up some change. Of course, there ought to be rules. No more than five commercials an hour. Students these days can barely remember their names. Five products may even be too much.

After all, isn't education itself a product, a kind of commercial for society? The lecture itself may be nothing but a prolonged ad for a certain prevailing point of view. Is there that much difference between endorsing Xerox and urging them to read Robert Frost? It's all paper, one way or another.

The MLA conventions, where teachers go every year to hear

papers about the English language, would be so much more colorful attached to a fair of new products the teachers could endorse. Think of all the freebies!

Post-Modern

A horrid new oxymoron has been bowling over the assistant professors of the nation: POST-MODERN. Everywhere you go these days you're bound to hear "Post-Modern" pop up at some point. We now have something called "Post-Modern Literature".

What is post-modern? It was a term originally invented for the convenience of professors who didn't know what to do with all the literature being written today. There were once these great writers, the moderns, they argued, who wrote great books. Then came us, who can't write our way out of a paper bag, so we must be post-modern.

Thanks to the nice umbrella of this term, anything that isn't great can be post-modern these days. Reactionaries use the term to mean the resurgence of tedious realist fiction. Marxists use the term to gleefully announce the end of those difficult and recalcitrant modernists, which could mean the beginning of social realism. Young people use it to cover up a general lack of inspiration in our times.

Everybody wants to be something, so why not Post-Modern? But how can one truly be *post* anything? Except post-mortem, of course, but then you wouldn't be around to see it. How can you come *after* when you are living now?

But that's precisely it. The term points to something more disturbing: people today don't want to live *now*. They want to live *after*. After college, after the assignment, after the baby, after the house, after the fact. They are even willing to be defined by an absurdity.

The truth of the matter however, is that there is no such thing as the Post-Modern. It's just inadequacy hiding behind a word.

A better name for the style of our times would be The Age of Homework.

As a survivor from the Age of Urgency, I am sure of it.

The Made-up Future

Now that 1984 is safely in his grave, the truth can be told: 1984 never happened. It was a literary year, invented by a writer and inhabited by suckers, I mean readers. Everything that happened in 1984 was part of George Orwell's script. If it wasn't in the book, it didn't occur.

It would seem that Orwell's future is now history, bringing to an end the arrogance that would appropriate a whole year for literary purposes. But Orwell was lucky.

Other attempts at future-grabbing will not be as successful because the future is becoming an increasingly valuable commodity. Think of time as real estate for a moment. You could get a chunk of the twentieth century dirt cheap at the end of the nineteenth. Jules Verne, for instance, a great spendthrift futurist, practically gave away half of our century in his books. Had we honored his claims by making our times look just as he predicted, Jules Verne would have owned all our best downtown property.

Prices have been going through the ceiling. You can get half an hour in 2002, for instance, for what 1984 used to cost in 1936. You could try, of course. There are thousands of fabulists who put in their bids every day: Short-term prophets in newspapers, trend analyzers, market researchers, science-fiction and fantasy-fiction writers. The crowds are driving up the prices of future time, but this isn't the whole reason for the scarcity.

More importantly, the future has become harder to predict because there are gaps in it. Parts are missing: 1984, 2001, and 2010, to just name the three more glaring. And another problem is that individual fantasy is now competing with corporate and state interest in the future. Our imagination is, of course, quicker and more limber than the cumbersome futurism of institutions—but they also have the means to insure that the future will look exactly like what they predicted. Which sounds a bit like 1984.

Maybe 1984 will be around much longer than we thought. Maybe no other time exists—which means the future ended in 1984. Maybe we live in the post-future now.

Forever Undercover

A friend of mine, the journalist Margo Hammond, was doing a story on a particularly corrupt union with a once radical past. In the course of her interviews, she was approached by an old man who whispered urgently to her: "I'm a Trotskyist. I've been undercover for thirty years! I was undercover when the Communists ran the union! I was undercover after they were ousted! I'm still undercover!" I don't know what Margo's reaction was, but when she told me the story, I laughed. The world teems with undercover dissenters. Some of them are so deep undercover that, like this old unionist, it takes them thirty years to come out and tell anybody. "What do you suppose he was doing undercover?" I asked Margo. "Mental sabotage, no doubt," she said. There are mental saboteurs undercover everywhere, I'm sure. In the Pentagon, at the top of corporations, in the media, in academia, and in the unions. What these secret dissenters do best is stay under cover. It's a full time job, particularly if you spend a lot of time securing your cover. That is, pretending to be the enemy. It occurs to me that the enemy might not exist at all: all there is, is deep cover. Everyone everywhere is undercover, too afraid to come out for fear of everyone else. Everyone undercover fakes the daylight so well that everyone else is afraid, which in turn spurs them to fake it even better. In the end, no one can tell the difference, probably not even the dissenter himself. What's touching about Margo's old unionist is that he still remembered that he was undercover. It certainly did not make the slightest difference to the system that he was undercover. It only mattered to him, as he waited for a glorious moment to surface. Surely, he must have expected kudos. What he got was laughter. And it is funny. The closets of the world are teeming with terrified dissenters. Meanwhile, nobody sits in the living room. The loud party going on in there is being staffed with the fake doubles of those hiding in the closets. The house is empty.

Beyond Speech

I had a simple but scary thought: What are my friends really thinking? I am beginning to notice a gradual discoloration of opinion, a kind of silence settling in at the heart of discourse. It is nothing overt, you really have to *listen* for it.

People say things that sound right. But you can hear a hollow sound in what they say, as if the words they had just spoken were knocks on a plywood wall. On the other side you can hear the emptiness, a whistling void. In fact, the more frantic the knocks get, the harder it is to mask the vacuum.

People who used to welcome important matters as grist for the mill, don't any more. It must be that the important things themselves are undergoing some kind of profound change, rendering them temporarily beyond articulation. Perhaps the new relations between human beings and their environment (the relentless destruction of the latter), the new threat of nuclear destruction (distinguished from the first by the automatic boredom of having been there once), the redefinition of sex roles (a number of verbal conceits destroyed and some energy re-distributed), the clash of economic ideologies (there are people and *people*), all these things may well be demanding a new understanding and, no doubt, a new language.

The fifties had hipster jive, the sixties had hippie mono-syllabism, the seventies had psychedelicized Marxism and Buddhism. But now, when we need fresh words more than ever, we get Valley Talk. And rap! Grody to the Max!

On the other hand, our intellectuals are making a fetish out of "language," in perfectly boring, grammatical sentences. Academics, who use language as if it were a sleeping draught, and avant-garde poets who treat it like a Babylonian idol, have joined forces. With the Dictionary proclaimed Emperor, and Grammar behind the throne, what is the use of knowing what anybody really thinks? I once asked a severe young scholar holding forth on "language": And what do the rest of us use? Meatballs?

With no new language to talk about things that will not reveal themselves in our customary old one, where are we to turn when the blossom of silence grows inside speech?

Certainly not to popular fiction, where formula-writing and cliché stand like border guards against any unauthorized thought.

And certainly not to highbrow fiction, where a relentless discussion on how best to market itself is taking place.

And most definitely not to magazines of general culture, which echo only the hollow speech we mumble ourselves.

And I would not (though I do) turn to journalism, where reporters, columnists, and commentators claw at the surface of public life scaring up more dust than a tractor on the beach.

And I would keep away most radically from the king of confusion and the master of subversive din itself, TV (short for Terminal Visions). A group of Christians in the West just had it revealed unto them that TV was the Devil, and they subsequently banned it. That doesn't surprise me. I only wonder when the rest of us are going to see it.

Even if the pretenders to the realm of sense weren't as numerous, the economy would suffice by itself to render most of us speechless. We are forced to speak the argot of prices and savings, food, taxes, percentages. It is enough to block the intimacy we once felt with the "important matters." Even the intimacy we once had with our own minds stands blocked by concern with objects and plans.

We are thus subject to a multifold attack on articulation: from our own futile attempt to keep up the din, from the demand of the "new conditions" for a new language, from language itself, from surrounding culture, and from the prominence of economic issues. Speaking the truth against the prevailing esthetics, over the din, and in spite of a sinking feeling, is no piece of cake.

But speak it we must, even if we have to do it from a straightjacket.

Languages

When people ask me how many languages I speak and I tell them, they are always amazed. "It's a sad thing," they say, "but Americans rarely speak another language." Some of them blame the educational system, while others bemoan the insularity of the natives, while others yet attribute the defficiency to arrogance.

All of these are in some measure true. The teaching of languages in school is a disaster. But my own linguistic education did not take place in school. On second thought, wait! I did learn one word: *okno,* which is Russian for window. I was in love with my Russian teacher, Comrade Papadopolou, who wore the first miniskirt in Romania, possibly in Eastern Europe. I stared at her in a daze for four years. Once she looked directly at me, and I looked out the window, which caused her to say *okno.*

It was worse with French, which was taught by a very strict pedagogue of the old school who corrected the misconjugation of verbs with a rap across the knuckles. In her presence I automatically conjugated anything that came to mind, and later, when I went to France, I could not keep myself from conjugating when the present tense would have sufficed. Once, in a café, I said to the waiter: "J'ai faim!" (I am hungry), and before I could check myself I said: "Tu as faim, il a faim, nous avons faim, vous avez faim, ils ont faim!"

But if French was bad, nothing was as hideous as Latin. Even the Romans, I am sure, had been bored stiff by the rhetors we were forced to translate two thousand years later.

So convinced was I that I was terrible in languages, that when I left Romania I considered pretending to be a deaf-mute in order to get by.

But then a miracle happened. As soon as I came into the presence of real people, understanding came to me. The small tasks of daily life—getting about, eating, and buying necessities—were the best teachers.

The first sentence of English I ever put together was: "Why don't you kill yourself?" Actually, my Romanian friend Julian put it together and he was very proud of it. We spent the day testing it on the unsuspecting. "Why don't you kill yourself?" I asked a group of loitering hookers by the train station in Rome. After much deliberation among themselves they directed us to the self-service machines at the station, which is what they thought we wanted to know. Ever since, I think of "self" as a coin-operated vending machine.

When I came to America, I had no end of trouble. People here just don't understand how there could be anything but English in the world. I was thrown off buses, scowled at in greasy spoons, and ordered out of 7-Elevens. But eventually I absorbed English just as I absorbed all the others: by osmosis. The language seeped in, making itself a home in me as I was making myself a home in it.

A foreign language isn't just words. It is another view of the world. "House" and "maison" are not the same thing, though they might translate similarly. Because of this, it is nearly impossible to learn a language without knowing the place and the people who speak it. Words come with gestures, gestures come with landscapes. Words are alive, inhabited.

This isn't to say that I approve of the disastrous state of foreign language instruction in America. Provincialism begins precisely with neglect.

Space

NASA's plan to send civilians into space in 1984 has me worried. They claim that they want a poet, an artist, and some unspecified others. They all have to be "communicators," according to the agency, and that worries me even more.

What kind of poet can they send up there? If they send up an academic poet, for instance, the heavens are doomed. He or she would be taking meters, rhymes, and surgical line breaks to outer space, and we will forever have a regularly scanned, severely syllabicized, gridded sky, peering sadly behind the bars of each line.

But would we fare better if we sent a free-verse poet up there, someone like James Dickey, let's say, who took the occasion of the first moon shot a few years ago to slyly praise the American war machine? I should think not. He might come back with a reason to bomb the Russians.

And as for artists? Should we send up a realist who is apt to paint nothing except the way he sees it, with lots of little stars and a detailed piece of spaceship tail? Or an impressionist, likely to mistake his slight blue headache for the deep velvet of ether? Or a minimalist, maybe, content to enlarge a single speck of cosmic fluff? Or maybe a performance artist, who can bring several colored sticks and flat stones with him, put one in the hands and mouths of everyone aboard, and make them chant "Gurley," very slowly and unintelligibly?

No, I don't think space needs "communicators." These sad creatures would only manage to take their prejudices up there. They wouldn't be communicating space to earthlings, they would be leaving clods of earth in space. And we would be stuck with their descriptions for years, the way Europeans were with the early descriptions of America.

The best thing would be to send into space someone already spaced-out, and used to saying, "WOW!", which means simply that things are beyond articulation. We could compare their cosmic WOWS! with previous earthly WOWS! and go from there.

Sit Down, Codrescu

Every fall I have a terrible dream. I dream that I, a man of nearly thirty-eight years of age, find myself at the back of a classroom in my old elementary school. I raise my hand to tell the nice old white-haired lady at the blackboard (who arouses an indefinite feeling of dread in me) that it is all a regrettable mistake. She looks sternly at me, frowning:

"No one is allowed to the bathroom until recess. Sit down, Codrescu!"

"But can't you see?" I want to scream, "I'm a grownup! I have wrinkles! I even have an ID somewhere!"

The words won't come. They are frozen in my throat, and when I reach in my trousers for identification I find only a prechewed piece of bubble gum wrapped in tissue paper.

I have no choice but to wait for recess or for the end of the nightmare, whichever comes first. If I'm lucky, I get through the dream without being asked any questions. If I'm not, the teacher asks me to do my multiplication tables. I do fine up to the sixes, but then I stumble. The class breaks into derisive giggles.

Luckily, I wake up. But I often wonder what would happen if I didn't, if I had to go through the full horror of alternating boredom and anxiety! All those days of aimless scribbling and futile efforts to impress useless facts and figures on my tender brain! I don't think I could do it. I wonder, too, what percentage of those poor children at their desks are not children at all but grownups who are dreaming and can't wake up.

Oh, come, I tell myself. School here in America is different from that damp jail of your childhood. All these open classrooms and visual aids, they surely must amount to something, no?

I'm not so sure. My old elementary school, located in the forcibly vacated building of an ancient Ursuline convent, was a drafty, ill-lit place that would have made a great setting for a horror movie. The classroom I suffered in for four years stood atop a catacomb housing the graves of several generations of nuns. A trapdoor under the teacher's desk led directly to the tombs.

That was the fun part. The mystery of the place made bearable the part I really disliked, which was sitting upright in my wooden chair in my pressed uniform, repeating after the teacher "A noun is . . ." "Six times eight is . . ." Only the thought of those strange labyrinths under my feet, with all their hints of treasure and curious past, kept me from bursting into tears.

I mightily resisted going to school. I fought, kicked, and screamed, but to no avail. Every day I had to put on the coarse blue uniform, tie the Red Pioneer cravat around my neck, and head for my doom. The red cravat around my neck was chewed down to the knot, a sign of distinction I soon realized, that separated the chumps who liked school and whose cravats were always immaculate, from the political prisoners among whom I counted myself.

For lunch, my richer schoolmates feasted on a hunk of raw bacon and a raw onion which they smashed with their fist on the steps to the yard. The rest of us contented ourselves with a nice bacon grease and paprika sandwich on black bread, and an apple. Lest you think us unfortunate and begin to pity us for not getting our daily vitamins, let me hasten to add that the stuff was delicious, and I even went so far as to make friends with a total goon and bully in order to gain access to his hunk of bacon. In exchange for a square of bacon, held to me on the end of his homemade shiv, I let him read my copy of *Around the World in Eighty Days*. He went on to read other books and is now a university professor.

From my classroom education I remember mostly the rainy days when, mad with boredom, I would stare at the dripping chestnut I could see from the window, lost in daydreams.

Startled from my reveries by some impertinent question by the teacher, I would say the first thing that came into my head. Astoundingly, I was often right.

I cut class as often as I could. Neither kindness nor threats had any effect on me. When it looked like I might fail, I put a small part of my mind in charge of memorizing whatever excruciating details seemed the most painless.

Would open classrooms and visual aids have made any difference? I doubt it. The way I see it, school is school. I am perversely delighted that I attended a severe, no-frill institution. Who knows, I might have been fooled into thinking that school was good for me.

Eavesdropping

I love listening to theologians talk: They tap on their pipes and finish their sentences as if they had all the time in the world. Nor do they shy away from splitting hairs or counting angels on the head of a pin. When I last dropped in on them, they were discussing a recent invasion of Mormon missionaries in the neighborhood.

"There were two of them, shy young boys. They must have walked a mile before they came to our house. I fed them some sandwiches and they said that God is fierce and will punish every sin. No infraction escapes His attention. Fire and hell are sure to follow every sin. They recited their grim lessons, abiding no interruption, raising the pitch of their voices and escalating the magnitude of God's fury every time I attempted to argue. Finally, I saw them on their way but couldn't agree. I can't really believe that God is thunderbolt-happy . . ."

"Well, I have no quarrel with God's fierceness," said the other. "What bothers me is this new tract I just got in the mail that says people were forty feet tall during the time of Moses, so he didn't really part the Red Sea, he just walked across. And I have another one here that says God made rocks and plants seem older than they are to test our faith."

They went on in this vein for a time while I remembered some of my own encounters with the Lord's newest shock troops. In Los Angeles, a few months ago, a scraggly Rasputin type with an underarm full of tracts grabbed me roughly by the shoulder and said: "You're going to burn in Hell, sinner!" I looked around: No one seemed to notice. "Me? What did I do?" He rolled his eyes up all the way to the giant billboard of Brook Shields's bedenimed behind over the boulevard and said: "You don't have long, sinner!"

Krishna's children and Moon's moonies, cruising the airport with plastic flowers, seemed a model of gentleness by comparison. I was not long for gentleness, however, because as soon as I landed in Baltimore, a middle-aged woman with a pleasant countenance rose in front of me and said: "Get drugs out of our schools! The Lord is watching you!" Lord, if you are watching me, I said to myself, You must surely know I have plenty of other things to do today.

No sooner had I finished my private appeal than two older gentlemen in golfing clothes cut across my path and pointed to me. They said nothing, but around their necks were boldly lettered placards that said: "Less Queers. More Engineers." That really baffled me since I could not for the world see the connection. I was very much at the end of my rope, however, having been called a sinner, a junkie, and a queer, all in the space of one day, over the length of the continent.

I am not wholly inclined to dismiss the lunatic fringe of the new militant Christians as my theologian friends seemed to be doing. In their lofty view, such aberrations were doomed to failure by their contradictions. But being a poet, I belong to a lunatic fringe also and I can see signs where others see only confusion. Why, not so long ago, on a miserable, rainy day, two Jehovah's Witnesses came up the muddy path to our country house and there wasn't a spot of dirt on their shoes. There is no way in *this* world that you can come up that hill without sinking up to your ankles in mud. Yet, there they were, shoes perfectly black and shiny, beatific smiles on their faces.

I used to live in California where, sooner or later, everyone is apt to brush against a cult. It could well be that all those cults are finally migrating to middle America where they are merging with existing shades of Apocalypsm (or Eschatology, for those who don't like made-up words). Whatever the case, whoever feels that the Lord is on his or her side seems to be taking to the streets these days.

The moral reform of the world is an urgent business, they feel, so why wait for anyone's sanction. Even the Moral Majority, with its cumbersome organization and awe-inspiring fund-raising ability, is too slow-moving for these folks. What they crave is miracles and, with the world being what it is, I can't say that I wholly blame them. Miracles don't come fast enough for any of us and when they do, at Fatima, for instance, we are not fully apprised of their contents. The man who hijacked an airplane, hoping to force the pope to reveal the third secret of Fatima, was crazy, surely, but his impatience is shared to a degree by the new street activists. Their overt aim may be moral reform but their secret hope is that, by making a lot of noise, they could force God to show His hand.

"When I tried to point out some of the errors in the Book of Mormons, they looked at me as if I were crazy," said the first theologian, tapping on his pipe.

"They should have read my book," said the other, "I said, for instance, that the revelation . . ."

I looked both ways when I left the house: It was raining and there was no one on the street.

Talk

―――

I often hear that someone is a lucky person because he has friends. By that measure, I am lucky. I have one hundred friends. Out of that hundred, seventy-five are friends who will not hesitate to cross the street to say hello when they see me. Twenty out of the remaining twenty-five are people who would not hesitate to buy me a drink if I was short of cash. And the remaining five are refrigerator pals, the best kind.

A refrigerator friend is someone who can look in your refrigerator, trying to find something to eat. And who can say, after finding nothing: "Your fridge looks like the dark side of the moon." I think there are few things more intimate than looking in someone's refrigerator. Frozen in there is the map of one's personality.

Contrary to appearances, which point to a gregarious and somewhat friendly character, I don't make friends easily. All my life I had only one or two intimate friends. These were and are people who like to talk intensely, seriously, furiously, and without any pause about anything, everything, anywhere, anytime.

My first friend like that was Alex in fifth grade, a kid nobody liked because he didn't like anybody. We walked from school the same way home, and every day, after a period of serious caution, we began conversing on a certain street corner that divided our paths. My road home went across a cobblestone street, his went up along the streetcar line. Across from this intersection was a church which had withstood six hundred years of weather and sieges. Imbedded in the wall near its roof were several cannonballs covered with moss. They had remained there to attest to the futility of a forgotten Turkish assault. I mention these mossy cannonballs in the old wall because they often figured in our talks. We would start talking about this or that and sooner or later we would begin to speculate on history, wars, and the past of our city. We talked until it got dark, and—in the winter— until we turned blue. My mother and his parents were not pleased.

Twenty years after I last saw Alex, we met again in New York. He'd left Romania many years before and had meant to look me up. But as such things go, he didn't have to. He knew we'd meet on the street. We did. After catching up on twenty years of news—which fit, amazingly, into about an hour—we found ourselves near the lions at the public library on Forty-second Street, where we launched into one of our profoundly interesting conversations about everything and not much. Two schoolboys sat there, suspended in a miraculous and timeless substance.

It seems that at all times in my life I have had just one such pal, with whom I walked the streets talking and arguing, and that this person always returns, no matter how many years separate us. He returns, and without any preliminaries, looks into the refrigerator, finds nothing, and says: "Let's go out." This kind of friendship seems slightly outmoded today, almost medieval, maybe the age of that old church wall. It reminds me of two monks with their arms crossed behind their backs, walking endlessly around a fountain, discoursing on philosophy.

On the East Coast, the lingering pleasure of speech is retained, a link, perhaps, with the old world, which is still in a functioning state. But on the West Coast, talk has been denounced as an enemy of true communication and the style is utterly blank. A talker is instantly suspect there. Monosyllabic communication rules. An excess of talk is considered neurotic and few true New Yorkers, for instance, ever last there. Woody Allen's terror of California isn't just funny.

My friends are all talkers. Silent types make me utterly uneasy unless they are listening very carefully. I prefer, too, the site of the dinner table as the center of gathering, rather than the vast floor of a living room where everyone paces with a drink in their hands. I never heard of a cocktail party before I came to America and, after all these years, I still barely understand it. Why do people stand up when they could be sitting down? Why do they talk only to one person at a time—and very briefly—instead of taking everybody in and participating in a conversation that feeds on everybody's opinion? Around a cleared dinner table, talk grows in a circular fashion until it becomes drunken noise. At a cocktail party, talk is carved painfully out of a block of drunken noise.

The cliché maintains that the older we get the harder it is to make friends. The ease isn't there anymore. There is something to that. In truth, the older the world gets the harder it is to hear anybody. That's more like it.

Insomnia

After dreaming of sleep all day, I finally lay down around two in
the morning and called on the blessed state of sleep to come.
Not a chance. I just couldn't remember how to sleep anymore. I
knew that my body was tired, that my mind could barely
remember the name of the body it was part of, but I couldn't,
for the world of me, summon sleep from its mysterious lair.

I remembered a fairy tale about a man who went in search of
sleep and, after countless horrifying adventures, found it in a
cave at the end of the world.

"Please come back to me," he pleaded.

"No," Sleep said, "I am mad at you because whenever I came
to take you, you were always doing something else and saying
'no' to me. Now I am saying 'no' to you. Go away!"

The man pleaded and pleaded, until at last, Sleep said: "If you
want me to come back, you must make me your wife. You must
live all your dreams as if they were your real life, and you must
treat your life as if it were a dream."

These were heavy conditions, but the tormented insomniac
agreed. And the moment he agreed, he was gone into dreams
and hasn't come back since. He is still wandering among
nocturnal visions, an oneiric slave of Sleep.

At the time, being a child, I was not terribly impressed by this
tale. Children give in to sleep with a kind of graceful and
unconscious surrender. I have seen children asleep on the mossy
banks of rivers and in shopping carts at the supermarket. The
only place where they sometimes have trouble sleeping is their
own beds. I sometimes had trouble sleeping in my own bed
because there was a monster in there. Perhaps, I told myself as I
tossed and turned, this monster of my childhood has found me

again. So I got up, dragging blanket and pillow, and moved to the couch. Alas, Sleep came to me no more on the couch than it did in bed.

By the time that horrible bird that wakes up all the other birds in the tree outside the window woke up, I was in the grip of a strange fancy. I imagined that my sleep had been stolen by people who sleep too much. If any of you are listening, get up and give it back to me, please.

The Solitude of Writers

Writing is a solitary profession. People see us occasionally in public and assume that we are always present. But in truth, a writer writes alone. What's more, he needs to be alone before and after he writes too. Marcel Proust wrote in a cork-lined room so no noise would reach him. Hubert Selby, a contemporary novelist, writes, they say, with his door open, the radio blaring, children screaming, chickens clacking in the yard. Between them stretches the whole of solitude. Proust's is the more conventional solitude, intolerant of the outside. Selby's aloneness is like a fortress he has had to make inside himself.

The solitude of writers may be vast, but is not like, let's say, the Great Mongolian Desert or the Hungarian puszta. It is not flat, monotonous, and consistent like the landscape of saints. It is a range, rather, a range on which sit not trees, but people. We do not really like solitude. We are doomed to it but we try to escape it as often as possible. We dread, cheat, and delay the aloneness as much as we can. But the terrible fact of it remains: to write we must enter the bubble of solitude like children punished to stay in their rooms. It is a solitude riddled with holes, that could pass for a cosmic sieve, a sieve through which flows the universe. And so far, I've been thinking only of poets, story-writers, and writers of *short* books. It is hard for me to imagine what the solitude of someone like Dostoevsky must have looked like. An underground cement cave lined with the graffiti of a million failed scribblers. The few years he spent in a real prison must have come in handy. In fact, many writers of long books come from prison or from academia. I think of Solzhenitsyn, who was an inmate, and of John Barth, who is a professor, to name only two.

For all that, the solitude of writers is not the solitude of prisoners. It is a largely populated place, full of the pleasures of invention, the possibilities of transformation, revenge, and dream. Interior space is stretchable, plastic, malleable, and often crowded. Paradox is our daily bread.

See you later. I'm going out.

Ghost Story

It is amazing what unemployed writers will do for money.

A friend of mine, who is a great unknown novelist, wrote love letters for a whole year to a woman he didn't know. The man who employed him paid a niggardly five dollars a letter. One day the letters will be worth millions, especially since the recipient found out, ditched the employer and married my friend. They are still happily married. That's a happy story even though he's still out of work.

A more famous case is the case of Anais Nin, Henry Miller, and Lawrence Durrell who, for over two years, churned out written-to-order pornography for a client they had never met, for the paltry sum of, you've guessed it, five dollars a page. (This five-dollar bounty on the heads of writers has to stop: Five dollars may have been a big deal in 1934, but now the basic unit is twenty dollars, please take note.)

Another friend of mine once wrote speeches for a politician seeking reelection and became so involved with them that he momentarily forgot who was running for office. He wrote his own ideas into a particular speech and even made references to his family and friends. The politician, who until that point had had no reason to complain, didn't read the speech until time came to deliver it. By then, it was too late. He read the speech because he couldn't speak a word without a piece of paper, and lost the election. The loser's wife ran into my friend in a restaurant and beat him up. He never got paid either.

Yes, in the world of unemployed writers there are all kinds of lovely stories. But they don't pay the rent. For all that, a mad dream possesses us all. We all imagine ourselves at the typewriter typing money like Norman Mailer. I have this idea that Norman

Mailer doesn't type words: He types money. Every time he hears the little bell of his IBM carriage signaling the end of the line he makes five hundred dollars. So it stands to reason that what he types are not words but cash, a subtle form of forgery which does not seem to have caught the always vigilant eye of the Department of Printing and Engraving.

All of which brings us to me. I have almost become a ghost. Now this may seem amusing if you are not as literal-minded as a writer. But the word "ghost" gives me the creeps. I know that it simply means writing a book for someone else. And I know that hundreds of people make an honorable living at it. I know also that some ghosts have become famous on their own and come back to life. But they are rare. Most of them continue being ghosts until they become very thin and vanish. I am not even that superstitious: The only superstitions I harbor have to do with life, not death. And yet . . .

The ghost agent I had been told to approach had his offices in an old Victorian building on Park Avenue in New York. In the elevator I already had misgivings. The ancient, musty cage of the ill-lit hand-operated (by a silent and evil man with a black cane) elevator was only a taste of things to come. The office was dark and damp with spider webs on the ceiling. The agent, hidden somewhere behind piles of dusty manuscripts, called to me in a hollow voice: "Come in but don't sit down anywhere! Every one of those folders on the floor hides a broken heart!" An appropriate greeting if ever there was one. I was ready to run. I'm sorry I didn't. Instead, I had to listen to the man's story. The ghost business was booming, but not for him. Thousands of famous people wanted their lives written, but they went to other agents. "And why, may I ask you," he exclaimed, "when I have the best ghosts in the industry?" He recited a long list of his ghosts. I hadn't heard of any of them. But as he spoke I had the distinct feeling that the room was filling with eerie presences. There was the mere fleeting of wings and a low humming sound, and I thought I saw several quick light flashes. Finally, he brought out a yellowing file and put it tenderly into my hands. "This is one of the best ghosting jobs to come along in years. I have saved it for someone special. It is the story of a man who was the custodian of the New York City Morgue for twenty-five years. During that time he saw many unbelievable things. When he retired, he wrote this book. The problem is, as you will see, that he can write little or no English . . ."

I opened the manuscript and came upon the following sample sentence: "When the Chief opened the body to look for bullets I was sweeping the fifth floor." For twenty-five years and for most of the book the man seemed to be continually sweeping. Once in a while he stopped sweeping and saw many unbelievable things. Yet, it was a most intriguing story. I handed it back to the agent: "I don't think I can handle it." I said. "Too much dust." Before the disappointed ghost agent could reach for another file, I made my way to the door, noticed that it creaked when I opened it, and bounded out of there. I took the stairs this time.

Only when I reached the hazy daylight smog of the Big Apple did I fully realize the entire horror of my adventure. Not only had I almost become a ghost, but I had almost become the ghost of the custodian of the *morgue,* a place which more than any other I can think of at the moment, must be *teeming* with ghosts. I had made a narrow escape. Shaken, I walked into the first bar and ordered a double on the rocks. Behind me I thought I heard a man say: "I think I'll give up computer programming and become a writer." I whirled around and shouted at the top of my lungs: *"Don't!"* He was taken aback, but for only a second. New Yorkers have a high threshold for the weird.

I have no idea what I'll do for money (except writing this), but if you need a ghost, forget it. I'm alive, thank you, and mean to stay that way.

Life against Fiction

Not only do novels and life have nothing in common, they hate each other.

First, there is the life the novel purportedly "comes from," something called "the past." If "the past" could get its hands on the author, you would be sure to see blood on the floor. Life, whether past, present, or future, hates to see itself re-arranged, clipped, and edited. Life takes itself very seriously.

I once heard of a very famous French author who returned to the scene of his last novel, in which the 500-year-old town cathedral figured prominently: Standing next to the cathedral he was killed by a cornice that fell 300 feet.

A very curious thing happened to me. I wrote an auto-biographical novel called *The Life and Times of an Involuntary Genius,* the first part of which was about my mother. Just before the book came out, I decided to check some facts with the lady since they concerned her. It turns out I had everything wrong. No, she didn't abandon me on an old chicken farm when I was two months old. No, she didn't name me Andrei because she was afraid of the Russians. But it was too late to change anything. The book came out, mother read it (several times) and when I next saw her she said: "I'm sorry about the chicken farm, the Russians were really terrible." Now everything she remembers is out of the book. Her own recollections have vanished, never to return. In their stead stand my yarns, posing as life.

You would think, from the above, that it's safer to make things up from scratch. Not so. I wrote a novel called *Meat from the Goldrush.* The action takes place during the Goldrush in the foothills of the Sierra Nevadas, and it concerns a family of enterprising Eastern Europeans who develop a bang-up business in meat by sending all the bodies of the dead Indians, trappers, and miners (it was a time of frequent casualties) up into the twentieth century through a time tunnel-cum-converter that changes human flesh into harmless cuts of beef, lamb, and pork. Twentieth-century America becomes addicted to this stuff, and the country starts slowly eating up its past like a snake eating his tail. History becomes circular and the millenium comes. Fantastic? Not at all. The place I had chosen as the setting for this business venture began to suffer from scores of eerie phenomena as soon as I finished my novel. The natives saw ghosts, barns burnt down, skeletons with axes in their skulls turned up on the dirt road, and a group of cultists practicing, among other things, ritual cannibalism was uncovered by the feds and hushed up because California had a weird enough rep as it was.

On the other side of the continent, in New York City, a friend of mine, a novelist, was starving. (This is not very unusual. Why do you think I'm writing this?) He decided to mug somebody since that is what everybody else did around his neighborhood. Being a writer, he decided to mug somebody who looked like a mugger since he knew that one day he would write about it. (He didn't but I am, isn't life funny?) He got hold of a switchblade and went to Central Park. A very tall derelict was walking slowly by the lake. Michael approached him slowly (there is an art to these things) and saw that the man was also holding a switchblade. When they came within a couple of feet of each other, there was the sound of a police siren. They both ran as fast as they could and hid together behind a bush. "Whatcha gonna mug me for?" the mugger asked my friend the writer-mugger. "I was hungry." "Well, see you later," the man said, when the police passed. "Hey, you wanna go look at some paintings at the Museum of Modern Art and talk about it?" asked Michael, ever the ready philosopher. "You crazy? I got work to do!" the man said, and left to do it. This has nothing to do with my subject, but it's a nice story.

More to the point, a few months ago I started a novel that I just finished. Being, by now, well aware of what life is liable to do to me, I decided to write equal parts of fantasy and "true" stuff, hoping to fool whatever it is life uses to get you with. I used an elaborate system of traps and detours. Every time it sounds "real," it's actually "made up" and vice-versa. I mixed names, places, and seasons so thoroughly not the best literary detective in the world could figure out where they come from.

Apropos of literary detectives, there is an amazing book by the French writer Raymond Queneau called *Icarus,* where a novelist hires one to find the characters who keep disappearing, one by one, from his novel-in-progress. Apparently, the characters, dissatisfied with the destinies their author prepared for them, took off to find their own. A man destined for fame and power opens a bicycle shop and is quite happy to patch tires all day. A beautiful, spoiled young rich girl for whom a doomed sex life and several divorces were being prepared, marries a farmer and settles down to milking cows in Brittany. The detective tracks them down, is about to bring them back, but has a change of heart. He quits sleuthing and marries one of the minor characters in the first chapter. With *him* out of business it's highly unlikely anyone will ever find out who my characters are and where they come from.

Having settled this, it was easier for me to put up with the other discomforts life causes the writer, such as having one's wife almost leave him "because she's not a character." Just to be on the safe side, however, I am changing my name and I'm not telling anyone what the book is about.

La Vie Boheme

Listening to the hushed tones of professors and the weighty ponderings of critics, one would think that poetry was mighty fare for the few, the province of the serious and the elect. In truth, quite the opposite is often the case. Poets are simple souls, with few needs. The buzzardry of interpretation only serves to obscure these simple needs I shall now enumerate.

First of all, a poet needs cheap rent. Poetry, the most sublime of all the arts, is also the cheapest to produce. All you need is a pencil stub and a wall. Or a razor blade and a rock face. The pay is likely to buy those materials but not much more. Between the cheap tools needed to make a poem and the miserly reward stands the poem itself, a magnificent and priceless object.

All the havens of Bohemia where poets have always lived have been paradises of cheap rent. Nineteenth-century Paris had horrible landladies and coldwater flats near the roof. Greenwich Village for a hundred years provided those same amenities with more stairs. San Francisco's North Beach was warmer in the winter, but the Great Earthquake of 1906 sent all the bohemians fleeing to Monterey. New York's Soho began promisingly enough, in lofty cheapness.

But poetry and art are contagious. There are always those, critics and professors included, who want to rub against them to catch some of their ineffable magic. The trouble is, when they do, the rents go up. When the rents go up, out go the poets. The hangers-on are left staring at each other. In despair, they sometimes produce their own kind of ersatz art to replace the real stuff, but it doesn't even fool the tourists.

Paris is now a museum. Greenwich Village, with the exception of parts of the Lower East Side, is a playground for the wealthy. North Beach is great to visit but be prepared to leave your wallet behind. Soho is full of gourmet food stores, art collectors, and little tacky-hip places that sell everything from postcards to lawyers. Yes, there is a little storefront with a gold sign that says LAWYER. Inside sits a man surrounded by law books. On the walls are watercolors.

After cheap rent, a poet needs a coffee house, preferably several, that serve expresso, beer, wine, cognac, and day-old pastries. All the cheap rent havens mentioned above were known by their proximity to cheap coffee houses and cheap restaurants that extended credit for the privilege of serving such clientele.

A literary café where one is known and greeted warmly, allowed to stay as long as one wishes even without ordering anything, is a basic civilized right. Which is why, I expect, only the cities that have such places can be called civilized. The history of famous cafés like Aux Deux Magots and Cabaret Voltaire and the Triesté are well known. In all of these places, poets and artists lolled about and talked without stopping. The standard joke about the tourist who comes to Deux Magots and asks: "Where did Jean Paul Sartre sit?" and the waiter says: "Right at your table, monsieur," is no mere joke when you do sit down in that café and notice only the lingering aura of the past and the incredible prices.

After cheap rent, cheap cafés, and cheap restaurants, a poet needs bookstores, both used and new ones, owned by pro-prietors with exquisite taste and a healthy respect for the non-paying patrons who like to stand in front of the shelves reading everything they can't afford. Such great bookstores in America were The Eighth Street Bookstore in New York and Books & Co. also in New York. In Paris, there is Shakespeare & Co., still there after all these years, and in San Francisco there is City Lights. Just how important it is for a poet to be greeted respectfully by a bookstore clerk, who is often a poet himself, could barely be expressed in words.

If all the above conditions exist in a city, that city can soon count itself among the fortunate places on this earth where beauty has taken residence. A city like that needn't be a capital of commerce like New York or a grey grizzly museum like Paris.

A poet's day goes something like this: The poet rises from a dream-filled mattress and stares fixedly at the urban skyline. Several minutes later he or she reaches for the ever-handy black-bound notebook and dresses (preferably in black, which Neruda says is the only proper color for a poet) and then heads for the coffee house. As the steam rises and the day inches toward noon, there are several lines in his book. At noon precisely he or she makes his or her way toward the nearest bookstore. Several hours are spent in pursuit of one's rivals and contemporaries. At around four o'clock, the idea of hunger appears and the poet begins visiting friends known to eat dinner regularly and serve wine with it. These necessities taken care of, the poet is now free to socialize, which he or she will do in the evening, when it is possible to merge with humanity at large, including the working class. Some days there will be a poem, some days nothing. But in any case, life must follow this course or there will be nothing.

See-Through

_____

I don't wear my eyeglasses in the summer because they feel like a brick on my face. A hot city brick. I don't wear contact lenses either because the idea of inserting objects into my eyeballs gives me the creeps.

You might conclude, rightly, that in the summer I am blind. I see hazy things, contours and shapes, and I use my hands to feel my environment. There is little to see in the city: If something looks like a building, it's probably a building. A bus shape careening toward you is most likely a bus. Almost everything in a city is pretty much what it appears to be.

It would be a different matter in the country: There, branches are really snakes; what looks like water is a wall of heat from a leaf fire. A tire is really a dog. A small shed is a horse. But in the city, no problem.

Since I am blind in the summer I write poetry in the summer because the greatest poets were blind: Homer and Milton, to name only two. There are staggering numbers of poets who have something wrong with their eyes. Among my contemporaries, Robert Creeley has a glass eye. Robert Duncan is wall-eyed.

At a party once, a little girl asked Robert Creeley: What happened to your eye? He bent down to her level and explained to her the whole story. I strained to hear, because I'd never had the nerve to ask him. I couldn't. In the whole world of people interested in his glass eye, there is only a little girl that really knows the story. And she's probably forgotten it by now.

So many poets are blind, cross-eyed, wall-eyed, and one-eyed that a particularly cruel man, who doesn't like poets, might want to invite them all to a party just to see how they regard each other. He could study them from a peephole, tracing on paper the trajectories of their gazes, and then build a gazebo using the angles for a blueprint. He could call the twisted result: Poet Pagoda.

The Russian-born New York painter John Graham has painted only portraits of cross-eyed people. There is something mystical about them, he declared. There is. And just in case you might miss the mysticality of his cross-eyed models, he painted mystical symbols on their foreheads and on their often bald heads. I could go John Graham one better and say that there is something sexy about cross-eyed people. I know a New York poet and playwright whose flaming red hair and crossed eyes give me the oddest sensation. I feel like I'm walking on water in her presence. I have seen her in the fall. This being summer I wouldn't be able to see her. I would know, of course, that she was a playwright because in the city something that looks like a playwright is most likely a playwright.

A friend of mine, an eye doctor, told me that the greatness of his profession consisted in being able to heal with the aid of the very organ to be healed. In other words, he sees what's wrong with eyes with his own eyes. Only a hand surgeon might be able to claim the same thing. My friend does complicated laser surgery and his eyes do most of the work. After a few beers in a bar once, he played a game of Space Invaders which, he claimed, is very much like laser surgery. He got all the enemy ships except two.

I didn't wear eyeglasses before I came to America. I didn't even know I was myopic. But I couldn't see the traffic lights across the wide streets of American cities, so after waiting for many hours at intersections, I went to an eye doctor. After he fixed me up with eyeglasses, I still couldn't see. It turns out that I'm color blind. Now I just cross when the cars stop.

The sudden wealth and sharpness of detail that poured in on me through those little windows were almost unbearable. I had always thought of the world as a soft, lovely place filled with sinuous shapes and long shadows. Now I had to contend with warts, scars, wrinkles, cracks, and deformities of all sorts. I averted my eyes.

It is well known by now that most Impressionist painters had bad eyes. They made the most of it. It is no coincidence either that the monocle, used so fiercely by aristocrats and nineteenth-century bankers, has become a sinister symbol. Those people only affixed their monstrous thing to their face when they needed to see very well the person they were going to crush. The gesture of the teacher who pushes his glasses up the better to see you is a chilling moment as well. Being better seen, under those circumstances, is only a prelude to being devastated.

If I really wanted to see, I wouldn't wear eyeglasses. I would wear magnifying glasses, or binoculars, or things that light up in the dark. As it is, glasses are only a compromise between imagining the world and trivializing it. Blind, I see all sorts of beauty. Enclosed in glass, I'm assaulted by trivia.

Danger Poets!

Eugene McCarthy, the poet and politician, said recently: "Poets are not persecuted in the United States as they are in some other countries. They are not imprisoned for their poetry. They suffer, what is, for poets, a worse fate: They are ignored."

When I read that, my mind reeled. Would the former senator like to tell that to Marina Tsvetayeva, who committed suicide in a Soviet concentration camp? Or to Osip Mandelstam, dead in yet another? Or to Nikolai Gumilyov, who died in a Soviet prison? Would he tell those poets and countless others that he, the former United States senator, would like to exchange places with them so that his poetry would be noticed? Of course, our "poet-politician" might be overstating the case. The only people for whom it is a worse fate to be ignored are politicians. Embodied in one person are America's two most virulent sins of omission, hence the strangely misplaced pathos. Even so, his words ring oddly hollow.

I have yet to meet an American who will understand why it might be necessary for a government to punish, banish, and sometimes kill someone for writing poetry. Sure, everybody knows that it happens in the Soviet Union. And in Poland. And in Romania. If well read, people might even know some names. Galanskov, Brodsky, Akhmatova, Pasternak, Mandelstam, Tsvetayeva. The list is long and the farther back in time one goes the colder it gets.

Successive Gulags, exiles, Siberias, deaths. The grim procession has nothing romantic about it. It is all tragic, brutal, and quite senseless.

Why were all these people hunted down so viciously? Their poems, in most cases, were not even political. What power they had—and still have—comes often from the *refusal* to be political in any way whatsoever. Did this enrage the leaders of Russia so much that the poets had to be destroyed? It is hard to believe. And yet, and yet. The doctrine Lenin ordered to be invented for writers is called Socialist Realism. Maxim Gorky invented it on Lenin's orders. Stalin, with the aid of a docile, boot-licking court, perfected it.

When I was growing up, in Romania, Socialist Realism was very much the prevailing dogma. It still is, though I don't think anyone pays it any mind. Even then, this theory was so alien to the Romanian spirit and our way of looking at things, we regarded the official practitioners of it with all the merciless contempt they deserved.

I was seventeen years old and the breezes of de-Stalinization were blowing through the land. The year was 1963 and it seemed to me that the sorry philosophy which maintained that writing had to be the instrument of proletarian propaganda and writers were tools of the state, was coming to an end. We saw, in the not-so-distant future, the end of the man-loves-tractor trash which covered the front pages of our literary periodicals. I was underestimating the regime's capacity for self-delusion. Even today, the front pages are covered with the stuff. And even today, the greatest poets haven't been entirely reprinted. At its ignominious peak, Socialist Realism did produce some immortal works. Here, for instance, is one of my favorites (condensed for intelligibility) from a regional Romanian newspaper:

A very good worker was noticed—partly because of his goodness and partly because of the flames from the steel pit which lit up his beautiful muscles—by the local Party Secretary. The Party Secretary was young, dedicated, and in her heart of hearts she had a beautiful dream. She dreamed of reaching and surpassing the quotas of the Five Year Plan in a mere two years. If all the workers were like him, we could do it, she told herself. Well, one thing leads to another, and in a short time the two young people were in love. Due to work and more work, they did not get around to talking for about six months, during which time the Five Year Plan did not proceed as well as dreamed. But one beautiful spring day, words flew to their lips. "I love you," said the Party Secretary, who always spoke first. "I love you, too, but I must tell you something," said the young man. "When I was a young boy and my family was poor due to the terrible conditions under capitalism, I was once left alone in the pig trough outside our shack . . ." "Yes? What happened then?" cried the Secretary, much pleased by both his sincerity and his correct thinking. "A pig came and ate my . . . ," said the young man. Needless to say, our Communist heroine would not let such trifles stand in the way. What mattered was the fact that he was such a good worker. They were soon married, and together they accomplished the Five Year Plan in two.

While we were thus amused by our faithful Communist writers, Alexander Solzhenitsyn was writing *One Day in the Life of Ivan Denisovich*, a book in which the terrible truth about Stalin's concentration camps burst on the world like a bomb. While the authors of amusing absurdities like the one retold above had steak and champagne in the Writers Union restaurant and drove everywhere in state cars, Andrei Sinyavsky and Yuly Daniel were marooned in the Gulag Archipelago for writing what they said was good literature. Undoubtedly, there is something demented about a society which so fears writers.

In an essay entitled "The Literary Process in Russia," Andrei Sinyavsky tells the story of a novelist who buried his work in a jar in the backyard. There is something in that act, he says, which appeals to the child in all of us, something mysterious and strange. To the authorities, however, this was a crime. And the author was duly imprisoned when found out. Would you like to know what this novel was about? So would I. But the subject of it doesn't seem to be the issue. It is the *hiding* of it that upset the authorities.

One could probably tell hundreds of stories like this, ranging from the ridiculous to the sublime. But the question remains unanswered: Why must people be punished for their words? Maybe, as some have suggested, the leaders of Russia are old,

superstitious souls who, at the very bottom of their cho-
lesteroled hearts, fear the magic of poetry. . . . Or maybe, as it is
more likely, they fear being ignored altogether.

In that case, Former Senator McCarthy had something there.
Only he had the wrong party. He thought he was speaking for
poets when he said that they would rather be persecuted than
ignored. In fact, he was speaking as a politician. Poets would
rather be left alone to bury jars full of poems in the backyard.

A Crime of the Heart

A few weeks ago, the police threatened to arrest my friend David Franks for indecent exposure of the heart.

In January the great Argentine writer Jorge Luis Borges, who is very old and blind, came to speak at the University of New Orleans. I believe that Borges is one of the greatest writers of our century. His stories are about the magic of dreams and of life, about the impossible longing for knowledge, about time and eternity, mystery and literature.

In one of his stories, a writer sets out to re-create Don Quixote by trying to become Cervantes in our century of machines. He succeeds in writing down the beginning of the Spanish masterpiece and Borges argues that, although identical, the unknown writer's text is superior to the original.

It is harder, he tells us, to write such a book in a world of telephones, computers, and police. It is harder, he says, to express the genius of the human heart in a world of increasing hostility toward human beings.

David Franks, in his way, is a fighter for the human heart, too. One of his books is called *Touch* and it is about the act of touching and the heartbreaking simplicity and complexity of it.

One of his performances consists of projecting on a wall with a slide machine all the mistakes on his typewriter correction tape. Look at these mistakes, he says, aren't they extraordinary? Isn't what we reject as true and as beautiful as what we keep? Isn't being human allowing for our mistakes? And he is funny. "My telephone bill looks like my telephone number," he says, and that is heartbreaking in itself.

He called me up and told me what happened. When Borges came, there was a reception thrown by the university and the

Argentine Consulate. David was invited. At the reception he approached the venerable old writer whose works he loves and said to him: "Would you autograph my heart?"

With the simplicity and humor for which he is known, Borges replied: "If it isn't a joke, why not?" David assured him that he wasn't joking, that he wanted the master's autograph on his heart.

Without further ado, Borges took out a pen and, after unbuttoning three buttons on his shirt, David guided his hand to the approximate location of that metaphorical organ. Borges signed.

They talked. People came by and offered their compliments, flatteries, and usual clichés. Borges kindly replied to them all. If the inevitable baggage of fame weighed heavily on him, he didn't show it. A few scholars approached him to ask questions about technical puzzles arising from his stories. A beautiful woman silently pressed his hand. That was the single gesture of the evening that moved the great man.

David stood by, silently watching all this. At last, he made up his mind to ask him the question that had been gnawing at him all afternoon.

"Maestro," he said, "I would like to ask you a very real question. If you feel that I am being importunate, please do not answer."

"I wait," Borges said.

"How are you preparing for death?"

It was a simple and obvious question. Borges is in his late eighties and death is one of his central themes. All writers speak of it sooner or later, but Borges has its presence never too far from the heart of his stories.

"Thank you," the master said, "I would like you to ask me that question after my lecture tonight so that the largest possible number of people can listen to my answer. You are a wonderful young man. It has been magic talking to you."

The lecture was set for later that evening. Borges retired to rest and the crowd dispersed. For the rest of the afternoon,

David walked around, happy to have made a brief and real contact with the great poet. Among poets, he reflected, things are simple. Magic isn't a complicated and occult science. It is simply the directness of knowing what to ask and how to understand.

Borges lectured on magic. He spoke about the eternal re-siliance of certain human metaphors which, although universally known, carry deep meanings. "Time is a river," for instance. Or "life is a dream." Those are almost clichés, but what richness of truth they carry!

Then it was time for questions. David raised his hand. Borges's assistant pointed to him.

"I am the man whose heart you autographed," he said. "I would like to ask you a question."

"Yes."

Before David could ask his question, two men on either side of him took his arms in a firm grip. "Are you going quietly?" one of them said, "or should the five policemen waiting outside come in for you?"

One of the men, the chancellor of the university, had been watching David since the reception. David considered his op-tions. He didn't want to embarrass the great writer who had, after all, given him such joy. "I'll go," he said. He dreaded making a scene.

Outside, five policemen were waiting for him. "What do you want?" David asked. They didn't know. They had been called to quell a disturbance. There didn't seem to be any.

"Indecent exposure?" one of them tried, reluctantly.

"Indecent exposure of the heart?" asked David.

There didn't seem to be a law about that, not yet. They had to let him go. But not before one of them said: "This isn't over yet," words typical, or so David thought, of the insecurity of bureaucrats in the presence of genius.

The Death of the Unconscious

Freud invented it. Jung populated it with weird Germanic phantoms called "archetypes." Artists dipped into it for images. Criminals used it in court. Men with pointy beards made money out of it. Men on couches with sweaty palms dropped money into it. Books about men on couches by men with pointy beards and books by men on couches about men with pointy beards and men on couches were everywhere. For three-quarters of a century it was a populous place. A gold mine for some, a bottomless pit for others.

I wonder where it went.

At its height, in the late fifties, it was in the common currency of everyone who had talk with their coffee and cigarettes. It was a middle-class possession, like a swimming pool. One had a dentist, a broker, and a psychoanalyst. It was physical, like root-canal and stocks.

Portnoy's Complaint was echoed by the nuclear family across the land. It helped relieve some of the guilt caused by the deportation of old folks into spanking-new nursing ghettos and old-age homes. Mom's wildly incestuous tickles on the butt and daddy's large Oedipal stick pounced out of it and were revealed for what they were: brakes on melancholy war baby's personality. So the old folks had to go, that was all there was to it. Who could afford both a shrink *and* parents?

The unconscious was a boon in other ways, too. By having it there somewhere at the bottom or behind everything (no one could say exactly where) you could always console yourself with the knowledge that if you ever needed something emotionally strong you could open it up (with qualified help, naturally) and have "a long draught of darkness," a psychic whiskey, as it were.

By the same token, you could deposit your anxieties in it for later reference, as well as things you didn't want to think about just then. The unconscious was a monster bank, unpleasant but necessary, a hedge against spiritual bankruptcy but, ultimately, subject to the capitalist laws of supply and demand.

That's all water under the bridge now. Because the unconscious is gone. According to a Turkish psychoanalyst of my acquaintance, every attempt to penetrate below the surface of anyone's consciousness these days produces nothing but television jingles.

To the request to "say anything that comes to your mind," the typical patient replies, "It's not nice to fool with Mother Nature." If he is asked how he is feeling, he says: "The more you look, the more you like." The earliest thing he remembers? "Reach out and touch someone." Identity crisis? "You're in the Pepsi generation." What does he want from life? "Double your pleasure, double your fun." Primal mystery? "G.E. brings good things to life." My friend is shocked. "America is turning 7-UP," he sadly concludes.

Another undeniable proof of its passing is that no one has any personal secrets any more. The closets are empty, the ghosts rattling there have long since joined their prop skeletons in anatomy classrooms. Instead of individuals hiding things, we have the curious spectacle of government and business hiding things from us. It is as if all our puny human secrets have merged to form one huge secret now in the keeping of the military-industrial-entertainment complex (instead of the Oedipal one), which might explain, in part, why no one knows what's going on. This huge secret, our collective unconscious, sits like the gold in Fort Knox.

There is reason for celebration in this. Human beings are in the process of being radically redesigned. It would be unfair to apply old European standards to the new creatures we are becoming. I do not lament the passing of the unconscious. It had already been trivialized out of existence by the mid-sixties. Psychedelics dealt it further blows. Self-improvement techniques bypassed it altogether. Television finished it off. We are new beings now. We don't need an unconscious. We *are* unconscious.

Had Any Good Dreams Lately?

"How boring," said Alice, "always asking people, 'How are you?' and always getting back 'Fine' or some other cliché." And so—instead of "How are you?", "How is it going?", "What's happening?", "What's cookin'?", and "What's the word?", she's been greeting folks with: "Had any good dreams lately?"

It's amazing how quickly the suppressed narratives of the night pop forth in answer.

"I was sitting behind a desk waiting for the aliens to come," said Linda. Linda is a twenty-five-year-old freelance artist. Her paintings are beginning to sell.

Claire, thirty-eight, is a lawyer. She's thinking about running for office. "I went to bed with a beautiful hermaphrodite in an elevator" she said.

I'm no Freudian, but elevator-bedrooms just beg for it.

Joanne, of somewhat the same socio-economic persuasion as the others, took out her eyeballs to examine because it seemed to her that they were entirely white, there was no pupil.

I could really hear Oedipus turning over in his grave by this time, and wondered if dreams were Freudian before Freud, or if they just got Freudian after. Certain authorities, like Dr. Francis Crick, maintain that dreams are no more than the discarded alternatives to acts committed during the day. Sleep just incinerates the rejects. This just can't be. Can Linda's aliens, Claire's hermaphrodite, and Joanne's eyeballs live and be rejected in one night in the same city? I think dreams are real, but the dreamers are not.

Doug is a café specialist in nuclear weapons. He saw himself pinned to the ground by pool sticks in his favorite bar, like a savage imprisoned by spears. His body weight controlled the trigger to a nuclear bomb. He stood up and the world was vaporized. If that was the alternative he rejected during the day, I'm glad he's still lying down.

I don't know what it is that makes pool hustlers more concerned with world problems in their dreams than Yuppies, who have a bigger say in it. Whatever it is, the dream state of the world isn't reassuring. After a week of the nightly news, Alice thinks that there may be a good reason for the old HOW ARE YOU? THANK YOU, FINE.

Invisible Battlegrounds

I went over to see a friend and found him in the driveway, pretending to fix something. He wouldn't invite me in because his wife was having a women's group meeting in the livingroom. I understood perfectly: my friend is from California, a veteran of the sex wars of the 1970s.

His strange awkward puttering was the only reminder of those great wars. There are no monuments, no wreath-laying, no honor rolls commemorating them. Pennsylvania has its Civil War battlegrounds and their monuments. But who commemorates the invisible battlegrounds of the sex wars? There are no Arcs de Triomphes in the kitchens of Orlando or the bedrooms of Santa Cruz. There are no ceremonies marking the anniversaries of role reversals, reconciliations, and separations.

Records of those mighty campaigns can of course be found in the abundant literature of the past decade, containing anything from radical tracts to *Readers' Digest* anecdotes. But archives are mostly invisible, buried in libraries the way my friend's strange puttering is also all but buried in his usual demeanor. The sex wars are singularly devoid of memorials. We are a forgetful society. Our main product may in fact be instant oblivion.

How many other, less important, more obscure wars have also faded from sight? Does anyone remember the passions of the Hair Wars? The martial Hair Curtain that fell between generations for over a decade, making strangers out of everyone?

Isn't it about time we commemorated wars other than the ones sanctioned by the state?

The Dismantling of Innocence

First came a new study showing that Freud was wrong on the matter of incest. The good doctor began by believing his patients' tales of molested childhoods, but later changed his mind and relegated them to fantasy. Until he changed his mind, Dr. Freud was only a neurologist. After he changed his mind, he invented psychoanalysis, a philosophy of language that dealt among other things with fantasy and wishing. But now, it turns out that his patients may have been molested after all, and that the so-called fantasy was in fact reality.

Does it matter? Some say not. After all, whether real or not, the only place the trauma exists is in the mind. Language is still the only way to unravel the knots. But others say that it matters very much indeed, because the focus changes from the individual to society. Freud should have invented a new sociology, not a new psychology. He should have been Karl Marx, not Sigmund Freud.

It is interesting then to see that shortly after this controversy erupted in the scholarly press, the popular press began filling with the most extraordinary cases of child abuse and incest.

In California the entire faculty of a school was charged with the sexual abuse of a hundred children, some as young as five. There is something almost mythical about the enormity, the deliberateness, and the callousness of this crime. It belongs with Grimm's fairy tales for its sinister quality. I marveled at the simultaneity of these kinds of revelations. There were scandals of this sort in Detroit, Chicago, San Francisco, but also in sleepy little suburban communities.

Maybe the *whole world* is a fantasy: why else would so much hard news follow an academic quibble about a Viennese doctor from another time? Why are we becoming so weak, in this most technologically advanced society on earth, that we must exercise power over the powerless? Maybe Freud didn't go far enough. Maybe fantasy is so quickly produced now that people themselves have yet to happen. We may be disappearing in direct proportion to our technological conquests.

The Boy in the Bubble

When David, the twelve-year-old boy who lived his entire life in a plastic bubble, came out a few days ago, he hugged his mother for the first time in his life. He stood in the world we all share and seem to get by in, but which for him was full of danger. David had little or no immunity system. For the first time in his life, he was free to feel the world directly, unmediated by the protective cover of his transparent womb.

What does the world feel like when it is new? Babies know but they cannot tell us. David could experience both the newness of it and the conscious knowing. But David's was a kind of freedom that fundamentally questions existence. His story was at once fairy tale and parable, as well as an unequalled and touching human instance.

Mortal danger came to him at the same time as his freedom. Inside his bubble, David was safe the way children are safe in the womb, the way people were said to be safe in Eden before they were thrown out for losing their innocence. To lack immunity is to be completely innocent, to be completely vulnerable. In our world that is a physical impossibility, and perhaps a metaphysical one as well. In his way, David reenacted the Biblical Fall in his passage from the Edenic safety of his bubble to the corruption of our world. But David's germ-free paradise was not a paradise at all, but a prison.

David was a twelve-year-old boy. A twelve-year-old boy, especially a loved twelve-year-old boy, is a person in a special state of grace. His mind soars, invents, imagines. He cannot be confined in spirit.

That he was able to move about freely for a time is an exquisite gift, made immensely beautiful by the tragic proximity of death.

Desire

There is nothing more selfish than two people in love, said
Flaubert. How true. There they go, hoarding up all that love
which in more diluted quantities belongs to everyone. Lovers
are shameless capitalists. If they reinvest any of that treasure, it's
usually in a grocer who sells them a peach, or in a waiter who
brings them wine.

Families are little businesses constituted for the purpose of
preserving whatever love is generated by lovers. Sure, capital can
be increased by odd windfalls at various times, but it's mostly a
holding activity. The incontrovertible fact that most people are
miserable testifies either to bad management or to one other
fact, which is that desire, which is the French name for love,
doesn't keep well when it's hoarded.

A productive "libidinal economy," which is another French
notion, cannot be capitalist. The national debt, which is nothing
but a lump of frozen libido, could be instantly wiped out by
civic-minded lovers. If they would only tear themselves from
each other to pour the stuff into the nation's coffers! But no,
they go about stuffed to the gills with the intoxicating currency
of the race.

Said Apollinaire, another French person: "Life seems so slow
to me. How violent the hope of love can be!"

There are three immediately identifiable kinds of desire, as you
glance about you. There is desire for another, desire for oneself,
and something called Greed, which is a substitute for the other
two.

Desire for another is the most miraculous. Most of us take it
on faith and it's a good thing, too. Any less automatism and it
would be like looking at the workings of the body without the

skin around it. Schizophrenics, alas, desire only their own divided selves. They *are* looking at the workings of their bodies under the skin and are consumed by the brilliance.

Outside of these there is only desire for money, and money is a fake Other, and a fake Self.

But no desire brings true comfort, whether it be of the first or the last kind. Said Rilke: "You can own wives no more than you can own flowers / whose lives are alien and apart from ours."

And the pain of wanting one's own divided self is hell.

The rest of the world flounders miserably about, spending itself.

The Private Rose

Our olfactory universe is limited. Dogs can smell a million things we can't. We barely have a language for smells. We have no arts based on smells, with the exception of perfumery and gourmandise. But those are small potatoes compared to our culture's chief expressive modes: the aural and the visual. We are surrounded by sound and captured by images. We have developed a sophisticated language in music and film. Smell, however, has remained confined to a primitive scheme of good and bad. I almost said "black and white." There are occasional attempts to raise the nose to art, like the one by John Waters, the film director, who handed his audience cards to scratch and sniff during the showing of his film "Polyester." It was a good idea because it is in smells that memory is lodged. It is in gasoline and pizza, hot leather and cheap cologne that adolescent America lived. The river of Marcel Proust's memory, flowing through the pages of *Swann's Way,* has its origin in the smell of some cakes he ate as a child. The smells of one's childhood are the road maps of the past. Mine were fresh apple strudel, burning leaves, tram tracks, and moss.

The smells of my growing up were just as distinct. Today the magazine I publish came from the printer. The smell of fresh print is balm to a writer's heart. The smell of one's new book is like nothing else in the world. Furthermore, all smells are interesting, even the rotten ones, of old cities in the summer. Every place smells different, and each difference spawns memory.

But what I like best about smells is that they don't lie. Smells rarely come disguised as something else, with the exception of certain deadly chemicals made to smell pretty. For the most part though, there are no trompe l'oeil smells. Pictures lie and sounds deceive. Smells assault and startle, and recall us places.

Questions

I have this idea that you should ask a basic question, hopefully a dumb question, every week. You should ask this question the whole week, of everybody you know. At the end of the week you may not be enlightened but, then again, you might. At the very least, you will have challenged some assumptions. So many things go unsaid in our world, we should make children and idiots a mandatory part of all decision making.

"In stupidity," said Emil Cioran, "there is a basic innocence that renews the world." And in innocence, we might add, there is a basic wisdom.

My question of the week this week was: "What does art do?"

I didn't mean, "Does it get up and mow the lawn?" but "What does it do besides lying there on the wall? What does it do to your head that your head couldn't do without it, for instance?" In one form or another, this has been the $64,000 question in art ever since art began somewhere in China. But it is amazing how odd people reacted when I said that. It was as if I'd rushed naked into their living room while an art reception was in progress.

For the most part, I said, trying to explain myself, pretty things that didn't do anything besides being pretty were an oddity. It is only very recently, in the last five hundred years or so, that art eased itself out of its religious, ornamental, or symbolic functions, to start roaming the world on its own like a singing vagabond. But since the outlaw phase is about to end as art is being corraled more and more by dealers, rich buyers, museums, plain speculators, and career artists, I am wondering if the question "What does it do?" might not, again, be appropriate?

Lame excuse, but then I don't like being thrown out at parties. Later, a drunk someone laughed when I repeated myself. "What does it do?" he said. "It supports the art biz, that's what. It stimulates the market."

That's what I thought. And I'm sober.

How Large Projects Are Born

———————————

Everyone agrees that the world is full of large objects. Sometimes the world is also full of large projects. Among the largest projects I can think of right away are The Russian Rivers Project, a plan to make all of Russia's rivers flow backwards, and the Star Wars Project, a plan to wrap America in a cocoon. Both of these things have been dreamt up by governments and are, well, pretty weird. I wouldn't want to live in a country where the rivers flow backwards. It's unnatural. Nor does it appeal to me to live inside an eggroll.

The big projects I'm interested in are ones that I dream up with my friends when we've had some wine. One of these, most recently, was a project for two paintings several hundred miles long, to be installed on each side of the train track between Washington and Boston. Everybody knows that what you see out those train windows is horrifying. It gives foreigners a bad impression of America.

There was a program in the Bronx where the city put decals of people in the windows of abandoned buildings. Women sewing on ancient Singers, pot-bellied guys singing, young wives screaming for the police, babies perching on one foot on the sill. Realistic things like that. Several hundred miles of that stuff ought to show America the way it should be seen out of train windows.

And another idea we had was to put murals on the cooling towers of nuclear plants, depicting Aztec rituals or some other colorful thing. We love it when Christo wraps up buildings and puts tinfoil on sea waves.

If we try, we could make this the Age of the Art Bandaid.

Pass the wine.

The World as Art

There is an art explosion in America right now. A new gallery opens every two hours. Dilapidated downtown streets are suddenly the center of chic new areas of commerce. Art is the vanguard of real estate, and a sure sign that developers and high rents are not far behind.

The art phenomenon is peculiar. In addition to the actual physical presence of the stuff, the artistic point of view is becoming the fashionable way to understand the world. The critic Carl Freedman, for instance, calls Ronald Wilson Reagan our "first postmodern president," and goes on to explain such remarkably absurd episodes as Bittburg, as "high instances of postmodern conceptualism." Seen in this way, many other things begin to make sense. What does the earthquake in New York have in common with Ted Koppel on television making TV diplomacy with the heads of three official governments and one unofficial one, for instance? Seen as a work of art framed by the same time period, these events are a bold collage of the perversity of old nature and the oddness of the new nature, television.

A few years ago we heard the phrase "art is dead." That was wrong. Art is not dead. It is the artists who are dead. Art is doing fine. Let me explain. Our postmodern world is defined by the great many surrogates we have settled for. Instead of wood we are happy with plastic. Instead of the one we love, we love the one we're with. The president is an actor. A large mechanized globe has been substituted for the planet itself. In the next stage, it is becoming necessary to personalize the fakes so that people won't feel "depersonalized." This is where art comes in. Art will make everything look original. We will soon live in a new baroque period designed by large numbers of artists. These artists, of course, will have to renounce their individuality in order to do the business of Art with a capital *A*. They will be dead. But Art will flourish.

Reader for Pay

A friend of mine has been trying to give away these books. First he put them on his stoop, thinking that people would just take them.

After a few days, during which no one as much as glanced at them, he put up a sign. FREE BOOKS.

That didn't do anything. People glanced at the sign and passed on.

These were not bad books, mind you. No inspirational literature or bound volumes of *Awake*. There wasn't a single book by Rod McKuen in the bunch. It was all quality stuff, things like *Selected Essays from Emerson to Codrescu, Remembering Proust,* things like that.

Once a girl with very thick glasses stopped. My friend's heart fluttered. She put her foot up on the first step. Then she bent down and tied her running shoe. You know things are at a bad pass when people who look like librarians are actually joggers.

Gloomy thoughts went through my friend's mind. He would have liked to reread Spengler's *Decline of the West*—but it was out on the stoop, waiting for someone to pick it up.

At long last, he thought of something. Under the words FREE BOOKS, he wrote: LINGER FOR A WHILE: $3.60 PER HOUR. That wasn't quite the minimum wage, but my friend's not rich.

Finally, people stopped. They looked at the books. Then they came up to get paid.

Still, looking was one thing. Taking the books home and reading them, another. One guy finally said it out loud: "You're only paying me to *look* mister! If you want me to *read,* that's 4.50 an hour!"

It hit my friend like a revelation. A new age is dawning. The

Age of The Reader For Pay! My friend slapped his forehead and immediately ran over to tell me the news.

I am overjoyed. This is clearly the end of all our problems—by *our* I mean us, writers. For sometime now there have been too many of us and too few readers.

Now things will be forever changed: for the paltry minimum wage we can have all the readers our hearts desire.

American Literary Circus

I stood in awe before the recent circus of American literature at Lincoln Center. Billed as a fund-raiser for an arts organization, the circus was a perfect picture of the current literary scene. There was Norman Mailer on the bongo board, a kind of surfboard with a ball under it, balancing for his life while reciting a poem. After years of teeter-tottering between literature and commerce, journalism and fiction, prose and poetry, marriage and divorce, politics and investments, Mailer was home at last. A bit overweight, and not unaware of the irony, he stood in the circus light a perfect creature of our times, a media clown. After Mailer, the circus gave up on literature altogether, and pure hacks took the stage. There was Ken Follett, the English mystery writer, juggling something that looked like huge lumps of cash. There was Gail Sheehy, the pop psychologist author of *Passages,* who performed something that could have been an acrobatic passage from pop psychology to pop absurdity. And then there was Erica Jong, riding an elephant, a metaphor, no doubt, for her career, which features a small-sized writer atop a huge mass of hype. It was no accident then that the ringmaster and chief commentator for the evening was no other than Liz Smith, the gossip columnist. As someone later said to me, in Liz Smith's column all things are equal: Mick Jagger's bladder, the latest Nobel winner, and someone's expensive fur live peacefully with each other. How postmodern! The folks in the audience, who had payed seventy-five dollars a ticket to see the show, were apparently delighted. Writers, no different than other playthings of our image-making machines, seemed only too eager to make fools of themselves. Gore Vidal, who is himself no stranger to hype, once said that in America writers are like Kleenex, disposable after use. Good point, but judging by this show, they've finally come up with endlessly reusable Kleenex. There is no telling how many times one can be in Liz Smith's column.

Inventors

Ed Sanders is an inventor of musical instruments. He invented the light lyre, the bardic pulse lyre, the talking tie, the toe drum, and more. He uses these to perform and sing his poetry. To make these bardic tools he had to study electronics, circuits, transistors, and chips. But when I asked him if he owned a computer he surprised me. He said No. And then he said that he wasn't going to get one because he didn't like the keyboard. He would like to see a keyboard shaped like an upside down salad bowl so that you can roundly caress your poems into being.

Inventors are notorious cranks. But I must admit that I've been dreaming about this salad-bowl keyboard ever since.

Alas, I know nothing about inventing things because when I was growing up we had a rift between the guys with glasses and the guys with the hands. Now I wish I hadn't fallen for that line. I wish my notebooks looked more like da Vinci's. A line of verse here, a quick sketch there, an idea for a flying machine after that, followed by a nasty remark and a lewd observation. In truth, poets and artists are inventors, but few of them apply their inventiveness to the materials provided by low and high tech. Sanders describes his light lyre as "one hundred garage-door openers."

Other people, of course, invent all the time. Behind those garage doors lie the projected bodies of a million weird things. The guy who built an H-bomb in his garage is no joke. His next door neighbor is building a shelter. Now, with the advent of the genetic revolution anything is possible. Sanders' bardic pulse lyre can be put in the hands of Homer himself, who may be quietly growing right now in somebody's Petri dish. What's more, the creatures of myth themselves can be made to come to life. Imagine the Cyclops or Medusa, telling their own stories.

Sanders calls his wedding of poetry and electronics a muse mix. Think of the muse mix of chips and genes!

Flawed Reality

I was in Berkeley, California recently and it was like walking into the pages of one of my books. The place had an insufferable literary air.

The Mediterraneum Café was just where I'd put it in the book.

Even where I had distorted the place, the street had taken on my distortions rather than staying true to itself.

I noticed the same thing about Paris some time ago. Every corner was either from a book or a painting. What's worse, reality had suffered from its encounter with art . . . It had been rendered slightly defective . . . flawed.

The incalculable damage wrought by art upon Paris is only matched by the damage art is inflicting upon New York these days. Uninhabited slum buildings are muralized beyond belief—to the point where they look more inhabited than actually inhabited buildings.

Where the distorting and wounding arm of active art can't reach, reality is marched upon by the art market and colonized, as in the case of graffiti art.

Where art can't actually turn something into a referential déjà vu, it literally covers it, as in the unbelievable murals painted by prisoners on the outside of the New Orleans parish jail. An enormous American flag a la Frank Stella waves over the facade, pierced by barred windows and barbed wire here and there. At Christmas, there was a nativity scene with the warden as Jesus. Right now the subject is Vietnam. Tomorrow it will be China. But never will it be the prison itself. Never the twain shall meet. If they do, the prisoners will just disappear. Who needs the world when you can have a picture of it?

The appetite of art for reality is voracious. Art scouts from galleries are combing the country looking for religious eccentrics and junkyard inhabitants who build visionary religious images from junk. It is becoming increasingly difficult for simple folk to keep their creative impulses safe from the business of art. An old woman in Texas who built a city out of tin cans claims to have shot fourteen video cameras out of her pecans.

At the rate at which reality is being devoured by art, I predict that the world will have a frame around it and a price tag on the lower left corner before this century is over.

Art Scare

What in the world's going on at the National Endowment for
the Arts? A little known and rarely enforced government directive recently came down upon the heads of our dispensers of
cultural moolah. It goes by the charming name of Admin-
istrative Directive P-732, and it means to ferret out "any
criminal, infamous, dishonest, immoral or notoriously dis-
graceful conduct; habitual use of intoxicants to excess, or drug
addiction, or sexual perversion, or sympathetic association with
a saboteur, spy, traitor, seditionist, anarchist or revolu-
tionist . . ."

After some of the NEA crew raised a hue and cry, and the
press started sniffing around, Chief Hodsoll said the directive
was being retired from active duty for the moment. But other
folks there aren't so easily persuaded. After all, we're talking
artists here, and everyone knows that if they're not anarchists,
revolutionists, saboteurs, or dope fiends, they are certainly
something so horrible they haven't found a name for it yet. Has
the government heard of *Expressionists,* for Chrissakes?

Well, it's downright un-American to scare people like that,
and it pains me, a recently naturalized citizen, to have to give
lessons in Americanism to the blue bloods in our mighty
agencies. But I remember, with a shudder, signing some docu-
ment when I became a citizen, that said that I swore that I
wasn't a Communist or an anarchist. "How about a Surrealist?"
I whispered timidly. The bureaucrat looked at the tiny print.
Surrealist wasn't on the list. He made a small mental note, which
is all his memory would hold. But, man, was I glad he didn't
know what that was!

Acting

"There is no more need for theater," declares a character in a recent movie, "because everyone is playing their roles perfectly. Fathers act like fathers, husbands like husbands, wives like wives . . ."

The actor, who was acting a perfect actor, was articulating something people would dearly love to believe these days. But I beg to disagree.

Today's children, for instance, do not act like children. They are being relieved of their childhood as quickly as their parents can afford a computer. Like the children of medieval peasants, they are rapidly becoming little useful adults-in-training.

Even the bums waiting in a long line at the downtown soup kitchen were acting suspiciously unbumlike. "What's for lunch?" I asked one of them. "The usual Soutine-like institutional meal," he said. "String beans and mashed potatoes in azure sauce." Of course, he was not a bum, he was an artist. And his fellow bums were all unemployed steel workers.

I remember a few years back the anxiety with which people greeted a movie called *The Stepford Wives*. In that film, perfect housewives sweep the house all day long and fix their hair. It was pointed out that in the near mechanical future all our human "foibles" will be bred out of us. But from my personal and not so personal observation, I can assure you that the Stepford Wife is a rather remote figure.

In fact, I rather believe that *nobody* knows how to act anymore. Why else would there be such a boom in classes teaching people to dress, eat, and talk "right"?

As for the theater being dead, I think the opposite holds true. We need drama more than ever. Perhaps what the character in the movie was saying was, "Everybody plays his role perfectly, which is not knowing what his role is." In that case, acting perfectly the part of someone who doesn't know who he is, is a great accomplishment.

Did I say that right?

Freud in Mask

My friend had a rapt expression on his face. He regarded his reel-to-reel tape recorder with the gaze of someone who had just set eyes on the Sistine Chapel ceiling. A great babble of sound surrounded me as I hacked my way to where he was, through a jungle of recording equipment.

"Can you hear?" he shouted.

Sure. I heard the excited babble of a hundred idiots drowning in electronic buzzing. I shook my head from side to side.

"You must be joking! LISTEN!"

I listened. This time, out of the buzzing eel tank came the indistinct voice of someone singing with a mouth full of barbed wire. Something like words half formed in the trembling air and then went down the hollow tubes of an immense din.

I resolved to find out what it was all about and pulled the nearest plug. The ensuing silence was shocking. It was as if the world had ended. Dying sounds hovered in the air like a rapidly clearing glass of alka-seltzered water.

I could tell by my friend's face that he wasn't used to it. Members of his generation have been known to suffer heart attacks upon the sudden stilling of the music. He looked at me horrified, as if he'd seen the devil.

"What is it I was supposed to hear?" I asked.

"Man! You primitive Eastern European! That was words you were supposed to hear! Backward masking! The newest thing!"

I'd heard of it. A California lawmaker had been trying to get a law passed that warned record listeners that the records they were listening to contained backward masking, which is to say that when played backwards, these records teemed with illicit messages. The assemblyman had personally heard the group Styx sing, "O Satan move in our voices," and Led Zeppelin sing, "Here's to my sweet Satan," on the backward versions. Clearly, a Satanic conspiracy seemed to be in the offing and the public had to be warned.

"OK!" I pronounced, "Let's listen!"

Relieved to escape the silence, which is worse than a cage where a young American is concerned, we plugged back in. We were listening to "Snowblind" by Styx, backwards. This immensely popular tune with its overt cocaine theme seemed hardly in need of other messages. If anything, it was over-messaged, so to speak. But there we were, hunting for its secrets, in the electronic Babel.

I listened hard. I used all my listening powers. And this time I heard something. Yes, there certainly was something there. I heard: "DENTON, FASTEN NORTH PAST!" I was quite sure this was a direct message to me although my name isn't Denton. My "North Past," unlike my "South Past," must have had something to do with a vacation I once took in Canada. Afterwards, I heard several messages, all beginning with "Denton." The most intriguing one said, "DENTON, LOWER LADDER FOR FARCE!" It was a Comedia Del'Arte sort of message. I imagined myself in harlequin costume behind a canvas backdrop lowering a rope ladder.

A few years ago, the novelist William Burroughs became quite taken with the ability of his cassette recorder to pick up sounds from another world. He swore that if you left the tape running in an empty room during the night you would eventually "catch" an other-worldly conversation. He offered several recordings as proof of dead people recorded unwittingly. I heard him lecture on the subject and tried it. And you know, I did get something. I got a rapid uninflected stream of talk in something like Old German. I never figured out where it came from.

This may have been only a tangential connection, but I always find lines of writing I didn't write in my manuscripts. I will open a perfectly familiar and overworked piece of prose sitting on my desk and in it I will find sentences, phrases, sometimes whole paragraphs that I never put there. I'm only mentioning this to show that the dead not only speak but they also write.

But another, more intriguing application suggested itself to me while I sat there submerged in a tub of vibrating electrons. What if the assemblyman's bill did really pass and all these records would suddenly carry his warning which says: "This record contains backward masking which may be perceptible at a subliminal level when the record is played forward." Why, people wouldn't even bother playing their records the regular way. They would play their fresh purchases backwards right from the start.

Everyone knows that the hidden is infinitely more appetizing. And when the secret messages come through, they could be whole chapters of Schopenhauer, Freud, and the poetry of Gerard de Nerval.

In this manner, we could have a whole secret revival of the forgotten classics and the obscure practice of intelligent literature. The world's great literature would pour in a great flood through the back door of pop music.

Yes, I plan to have my poems masked backwards in the lyrics of any bubble-gum pop rock group willing to take me on.

Whose Time Is It Anyway?

Nineteen eighty-six came to New Orleans at 11 P.M., not at midnight. The huge crowds gathered in Jackson Square listened to the mayor count down to 11. When that hour came the crowd broke into a huge cheer and sang Happy New Year! Few voices of dissent called out. A man mumbled: "That ain't *our* time," and another said, "The South gits it again!" The reason? Television, of course. Dick Clark, in New York City, proclaimed the coming of the new year on New York time. TV cameras pointed live at the crowd relayed the faithful deception to folks around the country.

Does time have a meaning in the age of television? I watched the Sugar Bowl and it was hard to tell the difference between the live scenes and the replays. Time was effectively stopped during the replays, and its substance leaked away. Where did it go? Where did the time when we watched the replays go? What happened to it? A friend of mine went to a wedding recently. It was being videotaped. As soon as the ceremony was over, everybody rushed to see the videotape. Reality had to be validated by reproduction. It is not surprising that we must validate reality by the traces it leaves. But what if these replays that authorize our perception serve in fact to undermine our perception, to overthrow the very reality they seem to re-produce? The videotape of the wedding is *not* the wedding *we* saw. It is the machine version. The instant replays at the football game are not what we, from our various vantage points, see. But how can what *we* see, with our human instruments, stand up to the supposedly "objective" vision of the camera lens? When midnight came to New Orleans at 11 P.M., it was already understood, by almost everyone, that TV reality takes precedence over human reality. Granted, time itself is a fiction, rendered more or less meaningful by the ways in which we regard its authority, but one can hardly imagine a crowd in, let's say, sixteenth-century France, putting off the New Year to suit an entertainment. After all, changes in the calendar once caused riots and religious wars. Human beings must not have won those wars. Whoever did, rules us today.

Grand Clichés

The grand gestures are back. All the grand clichés are being unearthed, even as I speak. Once again, in the salons, the sushi bars, and at little brass espresso counters all over the Western world, the Capital-Lettered entities are making themselves apparent. In the past two months I heard the words Evolution, Ontology, Meaning, General Theory, and, yes, Life. And nobody was putting any quotation marks around any of them.

Could it be that the reaction to social, philosophical, and scientific relativism, which has been quietly in the making for a decade or so, is finally bearing folk fruit? If so, this fruit does not resemble Charles Fourier's utopian pear, but some kind of medieval crab apple.

Personally, I am most suspicious of Capital-Lettered entities. They draw us away from the daily details of our existence, for one thing, away from the million minute murders of specifics going on in the world. If the focus is on Destiny with a capital D, does it matter if somewhere in Detroit someone is murdered in that most clichéd way, on the street, during a robbery?

I have nothing against the large questions. After all, we've been living with the Bomb for over thirty years now, and at least one large question hangs over us. But I worry about the nouveau gods of abstraction, things like Language and Signs. Are they not somehow discrediting the daily acts of our lives? Not everything needs a capital letter to be satisfying. The tyranny of meaning leaves little room for the simple joys of existence, while questioning most unfairly its horrible happenings. The imposition of meaning like the imposition of time, may only be a device to make us work harder. We may very well be extorted by meaning to psychic labor, just as the clock extorts us for capital labor.

Or maybe one of those weird cosmo-tape loops is replaying the 1930s, when a lot of big words were suddenly heard.

Reality

I have a friend who can't bear the word "reality." Whenever he hears it he reaches for a derisive chortle. I decided to educate him.

"There are four kinds," I said. "There is Reality with a capital *R*, which is the kind used by Communists and mystics to describe something out of ordinary reach. Then there is reality with a lowercase *r*, which is what parents use to help their children distinguish between fantasy and the hard facts. Then there is 'Reality' with a capital *R* between quotation marks, which is the satirists' version of utopian and mystical reality. And then there is 'reality' with a lowercase *r* between quotation marks, which is the reality of the relativist, fenced in by the reluctance to admit that such a thing could objectively exist. Your derisive chortle is the last 'reality', the chortle being no more than a quick set of quotation marks around my impertinent usage of the term."

And what exactly do *I* mean by it? In the pragmatist eighties, reality is making a sort of comeback. Recently, it has come to mean, "money," as in "face reality, kid, you can't go far on five bucks." Along with this kind of wisdom comes, unfortunately, a kind of piety. All kinds of things come in on the wake of pragmatism. News, for instance. No one in his right mind would mistake the news for reality. And yet, more and more often, you hear people refering to "the news" as if they were irrefutable and even intimate happenings in one's life. Well, naturally, pragmatism is a package: first you face "reality" (small *r* between quotation marks), then you find that it has a thousand faces, and then you stare into each one in turn, and that takes a very long time, and before you know it, you're old and don't put quotation marks around reality, lowercase *r*, any more. After a while, you're so convinced of the logic of what you've swallowed, that you begin to employ capital *R* Reality in everyday conversation.

After that it's curtains—and what kind of reality is that?

Do You Read Me?

People used to wear their hearts on their sleeves, but no more. They now wear them on their license plates, their clothes, and their bags.

In the old days you could look at someones's face and deduce from that what kind of person he was. A mean guy had a mean face. A sweet countenance, which seemed to hide a terrible secret, was precisely that.

In other cases, mysteries of gesture, ways of carrying oneself, the sort of clothes one wore, all these were sufficient clues to the observant person. Novelists and detectives had fun unraveling people this way. No more. The guy in front of me at the red light has a car that says LOVER.

I pull up to take a look, to see what a lover looks like. It's a young man in a fur-lined car with playboy bunnies hanging from his windshield. His fat neck bursts through the enormous collar of a black turtleneck. A nose, warts, a greasy smile. A regular Marcello Mastroianni he is not. And then it comes to me. Of course. The license plate doesn't refer to the man, it refers to the car. The car is a Trans-Am and a lover.

A little later I'm following a Ferrari license ALL 4 U. The driver is a sensitive executive in his early forties. A long-suffering look plays on his face. I imagine the terrible love and devotion he carries in his bosom. The hours spent away from her, which must seem like days . . . The ambition that drives him to rise above his fellows, in order to show her . . . The money he makes to buy her expensive presents . . . As I study him, the man's long-suffering look undergoes an abrupt transformation. He becomes joyful, demonic. I conclude that ALL 4 U is meant ironically, like an angry parent reproaching a misbehaving child: "I did it ALL 4 U, and look how you pay me back . . ."

One never knows. A license plate marked CHANT goes by. The blissful look of the driver seems to indicate that she is a follower of a chanting religion. But the cigarette dangling from her lips says quite the contrary. She might be expressing lyrically her appreciation of her Cadillac Seville which is like a "chant." Or she might be issuing a command to the driver behind her: CHANT! Or else. For all I know, she might be about to whip a derringer out of her purse if she sees my lips aren't moving in her rearview mirror.

A Mercedes license T BEARS 3 whizzes by. That's more like it: a nice family, probably, mom, dad, and a baby. But instead of these I behold three huge mobsters in pin-striped suits, smoking cigars. Or I think I do, anyway, so used am I by now not to take anything for granted.

Labeling ourself by car is nothing, however, compared to what happens when we get out of the car. With the aid of those seemingly casual garments, the T-shirt and the sweatshirt, we are quickly becoming a nation of books. Not booklovers, mind you. We are beginning to wear entire books.

I suspect that, in the beginning, the printed T-shirt served the same function as the personalized license plate: to identify its owner by his or her greatest wishful thinking. Thus, in the beginning, we had lovers, tigers, witches, bad dudes, rockers, spaced-outs, kiss-me-I'm-Italians, fly-me's, and so on. But the text grew.

From those simple monikers, we went on to entire declarations of faith, poems, political credos, stands on issues, and short stories. The Sierra Club is selling T-shirts this Christmas which explain in great detail and very small print the ecology of marshes, mountains, and deserts. They are also selling complete poetic declarations of interdependence, love songs to turtles, and short histories of extinct species.

The question of etiquette arose the other day when I had to

speak briefly with a young woman wearing an avant-garde short story.

I tried to read casually, the way you read a license plate, while conducting the business at hand, but this was clearly impossible.

The story, which started in legible enough print began to meander through orthographic and psychological thickets in stream-of-consciousness style.

The worst part of it was that after it reached the bottom of the shirt somewhere around her waist, it continued up her back and reached its conclusion somewhere around her neck, but beneath her long, chestnut curls. I felt that it would be most inappropriate to circle this young woman and to lift her hair. I left instead, terribly uncertain and very curious.

The question is: Are we becoming a nation of words, literally as well as metaphorically? In this age of communication, is literacy leading us to read each other instead of talking? Read this and tell me.

Obsolescence

The other day I tasted obsolescence. I realized with virulent clarity what it is to be a historical object, an out of date object, an expired product. I joined in an instant the huge dump on which the "pure products of America," having gone crazy, spend their last days. Hello, Old Car, You Queen of the Obsolete! Hello, Northeastern Industrial Seaboard, who once made things we barely remember! Hello, old lettuce, with Six-Day Shelf Life!

I will tell you how it happened. I went into a chain bookstore in a shopping mall and asked for my new book. Behind the register, it so happened, was the owner himself, an energetic, short man who could have clearly been a success in any sales field.

"We don't carry your book," he said.

"Why?" I said.

And now he said something so astonishing that I would have sat down had I known he would say it. He said:

"I don't carry your book because you didn't come to me before you wrote it, to ask me what publisher to get. I only carry certain publishers. And they ask me what kind of books I like to sell."

"But I am a writer," I mumbled feebly, "I don't write what bookstore moguls tell me. I write *books!*"

"That kind of writer went out with the Edsel," he said.

And so it is, never mind the evidence pointing elsewhere. The talk shows may be full of writers talking about their latest books, the newspapers may lavish attention on writers coming through town, but the sad truth is that these people have all, each and every one of them, been told what to write by the mogul I have just spoken to. The surfeit of writers in the press, on TV, and radio, is a huge mess of pretenders. I feel the way the queen of Holland must have felt when the drag queens of New York turned up to greet her in the Village a few years back.

I write *finished* books, that heed their own counsel. I am a pernicious type of individual. My line has been discontinued.

Just Another Day

Mother. What a subject. I never won an essay contest on the
matter, but I used to bring tears to all the eyes in the school
theater with my rendition of "Mother," by George Cosbuc. In
that rolling lyric, mother sits at the window, all alone, by the
light of a feeble lamp, knitting a scarf for her son who will never
come back from war. Around the fourth or fifth time the refrain
rolled around, I had them sobbing wildly. My own mother
sobbed right along, although I was plainly right there, in front
of her, not gone to war.

I don't remember Mother's Day in Romania when I was
growing up. Maybe they didn't have one, since most people still
lived with their mothers. The housing shortage being what it
was, children married and had children of their own in the
rooms they'd grown up in. Not only was mother around, but
also grandmother and, often, seated on top of the clay oven at
the warmest spot in the house, was great-grandmother. Great-
grandmother was usually the responsibility of the smallest children, who climbed up there with food and glasses.

In America, families have been scattered to the four winds.
The so-called nuclear family is a code word for loneliness,
distance, and a strange uprooted consciousness. Most young
people here try to get away from home as quickly as possible.
Old people are away in retirement places or nursing homes, out
of sight, out of mind. A recent court ruling in Florida held the
wealthy children responsible for their parents. It was a shock to
the young ones, unaccustomed as they were to any such responsibility. Indeed, the ruling was a rare one. The systems of our
society favor the young over the old.

In light of the cold facts, Mother's Day seems rather forced and hysterical, an orgy of guilt and commercialism. On that day, set aside to expiate the guilt of the other 364, an ocean of sentimentality engulfs us. Ma Bell, for her part, frantically pitches TV mothers at us, and rakes in the chips. All the moldy shlock of mom and apple pie and country gets rehashed for media consumption. Florists and candy-makers hinge their industries to this day.

For all this frantic ritual of affection, or maybe because of it, I get the feeling that something is wrong. In the novel *Ragtime,* E. L. Doctorow says that things went awry about the beginning of the century, and he cites Houdini, the great escape-artist, in this way: "Houdini was destined to be, with Al Jolson, the last of the great shameless mother lovers, a Nineteenth-Century movement that included such men as Poe, John Brown, Lincoln, and James McNeill Whistler." Since Houdini, whose mother died at just about the same time as Dr. Sigmund Freud's first visit to America, mother-love has suffered from a strange ambivalence. Houdini went to pieces after his mother died. He could escape from any man-made contraption, but inwardly he was bound to a love he never wanted to lose.

Segregation by age has the blessing of capitalism. Practically every day, a manufacturer comes up with a new product directed at some narrower age group. Childhood was invented in the nineteenth century. It did not exist until then, children being merely little adults. Since that time, we have created adolescence, and within that group we continue to find other subcultures; thirteen-year-olds today have a world of products and sentiment directed with pinpoint precision solely at them. Soon perhaps we will associate only with people born the very same day (or even the same minute) as we, and we will wear special clothes, speak a special language, and listen to our exactly simultaneous music. If youth ghettos and old people ghettos continue to drift farther apart, we will soon have ten countries. In all likelihood, we already do.

Our mothers, of course, are grateful for the attention we lavish on them on Mother's Day. One day is better than none.

God knows we all feel in many obscure ways that we have wronged our mothers. "All things are tragic / when a mother watches," the poet Frank O'Hara says somewhere. But beyond this feeling of personal regret, there is the vast neglect we practice as a society.

Quite likely, our mothers resent, too, the use we have made of them in our patriotic propaganda. Whenever their sons are needed for war, the propaganda machine goes into high gear to urge us to rise and defend the Mother Country. Most countries try to be Mother Countries to their citizens, with a few rare exceptions, notably Germany, which called itself Fatherland. The misuse of that metaphor, just like the commercial travesty of Mother's Day, is just one more instance of the unease of motherhood in our society.

Lure of the Impaler

When I first came to America, in 1966, one could live with
Dracula. When asked, as I usually was, if Transylvania was a real
place and if I knew Dracula, I would laugh.

But that was in 1966. Gas was cheap. Love was in the air.
People were rich in demons both within and without. Those
without inner demons (the unfortunates) could always look
about them and see the spectral figures of state power, the riot
police, the spies, the school administrations. In 1966 the Demons
Within and the Demons Without balanced and supported each
other. Since then the Demons Without have gained.

I first noticed the change in myself: When asked, as I usually
was, if Transylvania was a real place, and if I knew Dracula, I
would flash only a melancholy smile. Ambiguity had eaten up
the inside of my laughter: only its thin outline remained.

Never one to concern myself with facts (those enemies of
truth), I have always been happy to invent mythologies for my
birthplace. This is my motto: To a place rich in myth, add more.
Magical sheep, eerie mountain echoes, gold walls, sprites and
godlets, yes. But Dracula? Any of my compatriots could tell you
of their reluctance to claim this product in all its queasy post-
Hollywood glory. It's not like the Palestinians wanting back a
piece of improved desert. Our cinema-improved national hero
has not gained by the improvements.

The historical Dracula, Prince Vlad the Impaler (from the
nasty trick of skewering his foes on sharp sticks) hung on the
wall of my classroom right alongside Lenin, Stalin and
Ceausescu, and I remember staring entranced through the
interminable drone of my history teacher at the fierce eyes, the
pointed beard, the jewel in the middle of the forehead. Dracula

is our Washington. His accomplishment was to save Christianity from the Turks—by stopping them at Vienna.

You can imagine my sentiments upon arrival in this country as I was confronted with the blood-sucking reincarnation of my ancestor. You would be just as surprised to find yourself in the Carpathians confronted with a thriving film and comicbook industry centered around the figure of George Washington, the necrophiliac sheep god. (Progressive elements in the Tourism Ministry are working on it—but meanwhile they've hired an ex-exec from Disneyland to put hokum in our ancient castles. There is a Pan Am tour that takes you straight to befogged ruins and blood-curdling Dolby screeches.)

When my healthy, disdainful laughter changed to an ambiguous smile, my romantic life improved. The idea of sucking blood out of a person is an extraordinary aphrodisiac. It acts upon English-speaking people like the dust of cantaride beetles.

By the middle of the 1970s, I no longer took Dracula in vain. I became a fan of late-night TV, Bela Lugosi, vampire literature. In fact, the more I delved (at night) into the recent history of America, the more I found evidence of the fact that, just as the historical Dracula had stopped the Turks at Vienna, the mythical Dracula had stopped Jesus at the gates of the Drive-In. In other words, he reversed himself on these shores. Baffling as it may seem, the ancient history of Transylvania is the recent history of America. And I, by emigrating, had come home. I don't expect you to understand.

By this time, my smile had become a regular thin, chilly grin, charged with the implications of night. I remembered my childhood in the mountains, a mere knife's throw from the massive ruins of Prince Voevod Voda Dracula's castle. At another knife throw's away, in the opposite direction, loomed the bastions of Countess Bathory's castle. The Countess, known for drinking the blood of virgins, depleted the countryside of them until a huge popular clamor forced her brother, the Hungarian king, to wall her into a room of her castle, where she died singing ten years later amid a mountain of bowls. At another knife throw's distance (there are as many directions in Transylvania as you've got knives) were the ruins of another ghoulish prince. From where I stood (in the ruins of a socialist apartment building commanded by an ogre of a superintendent) I could see all the snow on the steep faces of the Transylvanian Alps like virgin movie screens.

My grin has now been replaced by the studious silence of a man with things to do. I am too busy to answer the questions, Is there really a Transylvania and, Do you know Dracula. Instead, I look into the eyes of the person asking. In there, I see a need greater than the need for food or shelter. I see an enormous vacuum, an imploring absence, a vast greed for surrender, and other questions, just as inane, hiding behind other questions.

The situation reminds me of a friend of mine who, during an earthquake in California, was conversing with a mental patient. "Did you feel that?" asked the patient, when the tremor subsided. "Yes. Did you?" answered my friend. "No, I didn't," said the patient.

Me, too. Some nights I feel it, some nights I don't. Sometimes the same nights.

See you tonight.

The Answer to Your Prayers

I have lived in Romania the first nineteen years of my life—and I have been in America nineteen years. I stand at the precise crossroads of this life of mine, split in two temporal halves like a metaphysical grapefruit. Another image occurs to me—that of a man standing with one foot on one island and the other on another. But I give it no heed. I do not feel torn asunder. On the contrary, I find myself oddly happy in my dual being.

The more American I become, the more American I am *asked* to become. We do not usually view ourselves from the outside, a condition described by the poet Ted Berrigan as "No one is a character to himself." And yet, one thing remains constant. I am Romanian, I speak with an accent. At the origin of all my human relations in this country there is this incontrovertible accent, sometimes *aigu,* sometimes *grave,* often hilarious. This accent, like Archimedes' support, is a mythically fertile point. It can be expanded as much as the imagination allows and the situation permits.

What do Americans see when they are looking at a Romanian? Three things: Dracula, Eugen Ionesco, and Nadia Comanici. In other words, a sex symbol, the absurd, and great gymnastic ability. These three reflect perfectly both the tone and content of American life at the near-end of the twentieth century. Namely, an obsession with sex, living in a world from which meaning seems to have fled, and the secret belief of nearly everyone that one has to exist gymnastically, continuously balancing on the edge of problems—and if possible, doing it with some grace.

Dracula is quickly becoming bigger than Jesus Christ, just as Halloween is overtaking Christmas as the nation's biggest holiday. Ionesco is the thinking man's Dracula: to be bit by the absurd is as liberating as to be bit in the neck. But without the comforts of morality and meaning, only one thing remains: walking the tightropes with Nadia.

Everything Americans see in us is central to their world. We coincide in a transcendental sense: we are the answers to your questions. But as a hybrid I contain both questions and answer. It's a balance I maintain most delicately, like Nadia.

Speak to me quickly.

An Anagram of Life

For thirteen years I was a stateless person, a man without a country, a creature from the twilight zone between legalistic definitions and then, on Friday, February 13, 1981, one day after Lincoln's birthday, one day before Valentine's Day, I became an American citizen.

We Romanians do things with a flourish: There is as much sense of occasion and ritual in these coincidences as there was at the scene of my departure from Romania over fifteen years before. Then, on a rainy day, an official dressed in the cockroach colors that become bureaucrats so well, gave me a paper to sign that said in melodramatic tones what I now have difficulty remembering: "I hereby eternally forswear my Romanian cit- izenship, never to belong to my country again . . ." Luckily, I had a sense of humor (tattered, it survives to this day) and it immediately performed a mental act with that piece of paper, an act I find ideally suited to most official papers. I then calmly signed it. How could I not be Romanian anymore? Could a piece of stationary issued by an unpopular dictatorship erase my roots and the unique pleasures of my childhood? Of course not, no more than a slap can erase a face.

Being stateless is a lot like living with someone out of wedlock. You have no security and few rights: the Relationship causes itself to be capitalized by constant thinking. It's a lot more trouble than it's worth. In my stateless state I could not vote, but I paid taxes. I could not own a gun, but I was required to serve in the Army. The worst of it is, I couldn't get in trouble like everyone else. Instead of putting me in jail, they could have put me thirteen miles outside the territorial waters of the United

States in a rowboat with two days' worth of Spam. I didn't even have to get in trouble for trouble to show up in my life.

For many Americans having a file is a sign of status, but for me it was an anagram of "life," which it is. There was stuff in my file even *I* couldn't believe, and I once bought a gold watch from a Neapolitan bum. There was, for instance, a poem I published in a sixties newspaper. Not only was my poem on file—which was flattering—but also whole chunks of other stuff from this newspaper, including one on how to make a bomb. While I was being interviewed for citizenship, the agent in charge kept leafing through this file. He would leaf and leaf and then he would come to an interesting part and go . . . hmmm . . . hmmm . . . I was dying to know what it was he found so hmmm-worthy . . . whole blocked-out episodes of my wild young life . . . forgotten deeds . . . bygone conversations . . . oats sown and reaped . . . Who knows, maybe there was even a novel in it. The thickness was right too, about the size of a French novel. I might call it, *My Life As Told By The FBI To Itself,* or, *My Life As Seen In My File.* But I wasn't going to call my agent until the guy was done leafing and I became a citizen.

In my own heart I felt American. When I smoked, I smoked Marlboros; when I drank, I drank bourbon; and when I rode in a car, I made sure it was a Datsun. I'm only kidding, pass the Doritos. Actually, I felt about half American and half Romanian, like Dracula. The American half felt ready to punch the guy out and throw the file into the shredder, while the Romanian half advised ancient peasant patience. This is, in essence, the difference, too, between democracy and red fascism. In a democracy you can rage loudly, in the other you drop your voice automatically. The Romanian half, floating wistfully about the melting pot, was melancholy. But the American half was setting off firecrackers.

I don't know if becoming an American in the 1980s is the same as becoming one in 1900, when the country was young and the possibilities seemingly endless. Being an American, now I have a price on my head, for instance. Stateless, I wasn't worth much to a terrorist. As a citizen, I may be worth more to a kidnapper than I'll ever be to a bank. Having all that gold in Fort Knox for collateral isn't all that reassuring. But could I have had the same name in 1900? Probably not. They would have called me Corkscrew.

In the evening my friends came over to celebrate. They brought me flag toothpicks, a stars-and-stripes painting, a six-pack of "Red-White-And-Blue Beer," a sculpture with the Boy Scout motto Be Prepared, a cherry pie, and a baseball signed by the whole gang.

That's more like it.

Miss Liberty

A TV producer asked me what did I think would be an appropriate way to celebrate the upcoming centennial of the Statue of Liberty. Have a ceremony, I suggested, in which you marry Miss Liberty to Edgar Allan Poe, thus marrying the two sides of the American psyche, the optimistic and the pessimistic.

Both of them gifts from France, I added parenthetically.

And if that doesn't work, what better way to celebrate Miss Liberty than to open wide the borders of the United States and let anyone who wants to come here come here.

You might want to dismantle the Immigration and Naturalization Service while you're at it, I also added, just as parenthetically as before.

This interview took place at Battery Park in New York, within shouting distance of the great lady and Ellis Island. Miss Liberty herself was shrouded in a dense ocean fog that looked like the nebulous dreams of a million emigrants. She was also surrounded by scaffolding, leaving free only the arm with the torch.

That prison around her, I said to the TV person, has to be the Reagan administration's immigration policy. The part around her lower body is the Simpson-Mazzoli Bill, and the stuff around her chest is that Supreme Court ruling demanding that refugees show clear proof of persecution before being allowed into the U.S.

This last one must make it very hard for her to breathe. I mean, how do you show proof of torture? Produce polaroids of bleeding hands? Tapes of screams? Signed butcher slips?

It was a beautiful day at Battery Park. The Cuban street singer next to us plugged his portable guitar in his battery-operated amps, and poured out a love tune in Spanish. Two black teenagers glided by in breaking moves. Two old men opened their Polish newspaper. A Greek boat whistled close by.

I continued my harangue.

Moldavia Up in Arms

I read in the newspaper that Joan Collins, the star of television's richest show, was going to Moldavia in an upcoming episode. Moldavia is a part of Romania, my native country. It is a beautiful, wooded, sweetly flowing country of ancient monasteries and gentle people. It is the home of the ancient Romanian kings, and a place of a long and sorrowful history. Half of Moldavia is today part of the Soviet Union, a World War II land-grab that shows like an open wound along the Tissa River.

I became very excited about seeing even a bit of my old country. Even with Alexis covering most of the screen, I might still glimpse something: the cupolas of the Voronetz monastery, the old oaks . . . Around eight o'clock I settled down with my enemy. I was even ready, for the coming hour, to forgive television its malevolent and relentless destruction of the human mind in our time. After five hundred changes of clothes, Joan Collins hit the Moldavian border. The place looked suspiciously like the San Bernardino county border, the orange groves and all. Before I could scream an obscenity, a dozen Lybian terrorists surrounded Joan Collins, who was dressed as a nun. They must have been left over from ABC's last terrorist movie-of-the-week. These Lybian-Moldavians then whisked the nun's traveling companion across San Berdoo's orange groves through a Moldavia identified by the word MOLDAVIA flashing across the screen. Now I wasn't simply outraged by the flagrant stupidity, something which, after all, I've come to expect from the medium. It wasn't even the fact that whenever I compromise with the idiot box, I'm forcefully reminded of my reasons for reviling it in the first place. No, it wasn't that. It was the simple realization of sheer callousness. There might not be many Romanians around.

Not any named Nielsen, in any case. But you would think that somewhere in the tiny brains of people in charge of our visual control, the minimal thought of consulting a real Romanian could have dawned. For a hundred bucks they could have had their facts straight, and gladdened a few hearts. Instead, not a penny of the multimillion-dollar puke fest went even to a modicum of truth.

The New Geography

My friend Sasha is studying for his citizenship. American history bewilders him. But it's nothing compared to geography. He comes from a country where most places were named after men. History is writ large in the names of cities. When Petrograd changed its name to Leningrad you could hear the wheel of time turning.

But what to make of American geography, with its record of rapid conquests and waves of migration?

Mississippi, Tennessee, Michigan, Kentucky, Cincinnati, Chattanooga, Winemucca, Tallahassee were all named by the Indians. But places like Omaha, Sioux City, Cheyenne, Kansas City and Chipewa Falls were named by white people *after* Indians.

The English named New York, Virginia, and the Carolinas after places in the Old World. Likewise, the French, with New Orleans, Louisiana, Detroit, Saint Louis, Dubuque, and Baton Rouge. And then you have the Spanish in Saint Augustine, San Francisco, Los Angeles, El Paso, Las Vegas, and San Antonio.

Then there are towns named after people: Bismarck, Jacksonville, Charleston, Washington, Baltimore, Montgomery, Houston, Charlotte. And there are people named after places, Tennessee Williams, Judy Chicago, Joe Montana, and John Denver.

All this wouldn't baffle Sasha so much if it weren't for all the new towns he drives through when he goes to visit friends in the next state. He passes through Toshiba Falls, a charming little town just west of New Nissan. When he gets there, he takes the shuttle to Sonyopolis or Toyota Ferry, and spends a few days with his friends at Sonic Inn, where they eat hamburgers and dance at the Chip Dust Disco. Sometimes they drive to Silicon Valley for sushi.

It's really quite simple, Sasha. Geography is only a matter of time.

A Hero of Our Time

1. *Looking*

Antim was looking for the center of town. He thought he found it by the train station. He leaned against a wall to watch people. He was wearing tight jeans. A car stopped and a guy propositioned him. Antim doesn't know English but the gesture was clear enough. Now he's angry. "In Romania," he says, "all the queers are killed."

We walk through Baltimore's Inner Harbor, talking. Baltimore's showpiece doesn't interest him. In Little Italy he shows some interest in the outside. Something familiar, maybe the clothes on the clotheslines.

The Catholic charity that is sponsoring him has installed him in a room in an Eastern Avenue rowhouse. He's been living there almost twenty days now and has already worn out one pair of shoes, walking.

In Romania he was the curator of a small folk museum in a small mountain city. He attended art school in a provincial capital, and calls himself an artist. In his first ten days in America he looked for the "Art Center." Romania abounds in centers of art: the Ministry of Culture, the Artists' Union, the Art House. Following that scheme of things, he visited several galleries that were frightfully unconnected to any visible "center." At long last, he found himself at the Maryland Arts Council on Mulberry Street. Here he met Linda Vlasak.

Mrs. Vlasak understood: she is a Czech who came here in the fifties. She offered Antim some help with materials. She also tried to explain things to him. Here, she told him, you take your art to galleries, to fairs, to contests. You paint on the street if you want quick money, and sell to tourists.

Antim didn't say anything. He had only contempt for such anarchy. In Romania, an artist is a carefully nurtured product of his society. He goes to art school, is authorized, is employed in some art-bureaucratic capacity, and is then brought slowly along by his elders, with a painting in a State-farm show, a drawing in a traveling factory exhibit. All works are purchased by the State. There are no private showings, no private collectors. There are no walls to paint, no unofficial commissions.

Mrs. Vlasak puts it this way: "He has no concept of freedom. Freedom is terrifying. There are suddenly all these options. The paternalistic umbrella is removed."

I met Antim in the lobby of the Arts Council. I took him cautiously on. A fellow Romanian, an artist. Terrific. But you never know: the long arm of the Commie police sometimes holds a paint brush. Of sturdy build, with a fine mustache, a gold chain around his neck, ten years younger than me—he seems too perfect, stylized even. I am curious to hear how things are in Romania now. He tells me.

You can buy anything or anybody for a pack of Kent cigarettes. The villages are deserted, there is no food in the countryside. There are breadlines in every city. Food rationing and coupons have reappeared. There is nothing in stores except cans. The lights in the cities go out at 10 P.M. There is no nightlife. An average monthly salary buys a pair of black-market bluejeans. There is a law against unemployment. Anyone found unemployed goes to prison. The prisons are full of young people.

Under these circumstances, I ask, what kind of art is being made? Social Realism?

Not at all, Antim says vehemently. Many artists copy modern trends and styles from forbidden foreign magazines. Everything is highly elitist, intellectual, refined, and unconnected with the life of the country. Art for art's sake is the only philosophy. That goes for literature, theater, and the cinema, as well.

What do people think? I ask.

Escape, says Antim. The only thing on their minds is how to

get out. They will do anything. Several men were found hiding in the smokestacks of a ship at Constantza. They were dead from the smoke. At the Yugoslav border they found a tree that was a slingshot. People catapulted out of it across the border. They hide in foreigners' car trunks, they wriggle through mine fields, they make gliders from scarce paper bags.

How did you get out?

Through art, he says.

2. *The Escape*

The way Antim tells it, he had this idea for two years before he put it into practice. He befriended a worker in the railway yard at Cluj. The two of them carefully studied the trains leaving the country. Then they constructed a tin roof for the ceiling of a Vienna-bound car train. It looked exactly like the ceiling. But between their ceiling and the real ceiling there was a crawl space sufficient for the two of them to wrap themselves around each other. They traveled like that for two and a half days, eating chocolate bars in the dark. They listened to border guards check passports, they held their breaths while the passengers slept.

Antim tells of his escape in great detail. This is quite unlike his other tales. About his life before the escape he is vague. He prefers to analyze things. He talks about "culture," "society," "fragmentation."

I congratulate him on his cleverness and ask him if he is familiar with the work of the American realists, artists like George Segal who create startling imitations of reality. He is not. I tell him that his escape is a work of art and the false ceiling would be a fine piece to exhibit.

He says nothing. Art for him is something else. It is not on the same plane as life.

"I know these Russian artists," Mrs. Vlasak tells me, "who took five years to tell what they honestly thought. Oh, they told you plenty, but it was usually the opposite of what they really believed. There is a duplicity they bring with them from those countries, a form of self-protection really, and they continue using it even when there is no reason to. I explained to them that here a person's trustworthiness is their most valuable asset. Statements are not met with automatic skepticism. People do not feel compelled to play games with face value. Everybody believes what you say. In America even the Mafia is honest—among themselves, of course."

There is something else about Antim, however. He is far from being in clear focus. Maybe it is only the fact that he and I are from two different generations. I left Romania at the height of a liberal and relatively affluent period. We were optimistic, enthusiastic, guileless. We were almost Americans in some sense. Antim is dour. In ten years culture has been debased, cynicism is pervasive, there is little that hasn't been institutionalized. His generation believes in nothing.

3. *The Death of Art*

Antim doesn't know what to do. He has no money. He receives food stamps and the room rent. But he would like some work. The sketches he shows me are mediocre. Student work. A charcoal-drawn jug. Part of a country fence. Attempts for the most part at a pseudo-folkloric stylization. He did have some work painting a house for two days: with the money he bought the gold-chain around his neck. He is proud of it. "In Romania," he says, "you work a year for this."

We pass a gun store. He is astounded. You mean, anyone can buy a gun here? Yes, I say. We walk into the store and I watch his astonished wonder at being able to hold one revolver after another. He is intoxicated with pleasure. He weighs them, he rolls them, he twirls the barrel of a six-shooter.

Back on the street, he becomes greatly animated. He tells me about making a previous attempt at escape by apprenticing himself to an old fresco painter at a church near the border. He mixed the egg temperas for the old man. But one day, the police showed up and he got out in the nick of time.

Art keeps coming up. And oddly, there is more of a gulf between us than I previously thought. I thought, at first, that I recognized myself in Antim. Both of us came here young, penniless, ambitious. But as we talk I realize that time is merciless and it divides us more categorically than if we were from different planets. As a child of the sixties, I still see the world hopefully, with an enthusiasm born of a time when possibilities seemed limitless. Even in Romania, we would be similarly divided. You would not recognize Romania now, says Antim. Misery. Drunkenness. Prostitution. Fear. It is true. I probably wouldn't. When I came here I traveled thousands of miles telling my story, bathing in the *esprit du temps*. Antim can't. He sees six million unemployed people. Anarchy. The lack of a center. He is a man of the eighties, a hero maybe (for trying to escape somewhere, anywhere) but he has little to look forward to. And doesn't want to, anyway. In Romania he was condemned to a numbing conformity which eventually would have transformed him into a listless and fearful accomplice. Here, he arrives at a time of suspicion, xenophobia, unemployment. His expectations reflect it. If someone had asked me, in the 1960s, what I wanted from America, I would have said: Recognize me as the greatest American poet! (And I couldn't even speak English.) But now when I ask Antim, he says: "A little work, only a little work. A few days' work."

Escape is the art of our time but there is no escape from time. Art may very well be dead.

Hair

I don't know what it is about hair that drives people stark raving mad. A possible explanation, offered gratis by a hitchhiker once, is that hair is really nerves that grow out of the body. Hence, the more hair you have the more nervous you are, which would make bald people islands of serenity. My grandmother, who knew everything, exhorted me to push my hair up as far away from my forehead as possible because if I didn't, hair would grow on my forehead. I used to wake up in a cold sweat, sure that I had turned into a werewolf during the night. In the 1960s, I found my Delilah in the person of a Polish barber in the business-starved Lower East Side of New York, where anybody under thirty who didn't have long hair was either a tourist or a cop. I don't know what possessed me to enter the haunted emptiness of that barber shop, but whatever it was, I had reason to regret it. The man had been staring out of his dusty window for years before I walked in. His tools were rusted, his magazines ancient, and the ravenous light of madness shone from his eyes. When he captured me, he locked the door, tied me to the chair and, in two wide swaths, cut a path all the way down to my scalp. I was forced to wear a hat for two months.

Now that the great Hair Wars of the sixties and seventies seem to have receded, leaving behind only a handful of memories like curly locks on the floor of a barber shop at closing time, perhaps we can look calmly at the phenomenon. After all, hair is only a movie now and not the public threat it once was.

I first realized the power of hair shortly after I arrived in Detroit in 1966 and was shown by my guide, not the General Motors building or a famous mafioso, but a man named Jerry Younkins, a poet who had the longest hair in the Midwest, proudly uncut for fifteen years. Jerry's hair was amazing, hanging as it did down to the backs of his knees, a triumphant waterfall which made it difficult for him to stand, though he did stand, and proudly, a walking generational and political statement in the heart of Motor City.

Freshly arrived from behind the Iron Curtain, I became aware that a Hair Curtain was falling suddenly between generations with a ferociousness only dimly graspable now. Unlike the Iron Curtain, however, the Hair Curtain cut right across political and geographical boundaries, equally at home in Prague and Chicago. The passions aroused by ideology almost paled next to those aroused by hair. Municipalities, states, and countries closed their borders to long hair, and half the world began chasing the other half with scissors, razor blades, and, at times, machine guns. For a time, it seemed safe to assume that long hair stood for something, though no one could say exactly what. The police assumed it stood for drugs and anarchy. We assumed it stood for freedom.

The other day I came upon an early Beatles album on the cover of which four clean-cut young men shine forth with a wholesomeness that makes it hard to see what all the fuss was about. Their hair, short by today's standards, seems hardly the thing to start a war. And yet, like a mighty river traceable to some puny spring, the great Hair Wars have their source in this photo. It makes me wonder if the whole thing wasn't some dream from which, awakened, the dreamer throws himself in the shower trying to forget. For the Beatles, long hair turned out to be money in the bank. For others, it was something in the nature of a command from that elusive beast the French call *esprit du siecle:* "Grow your hair long and go forth into the world, young man!" For some, it might have been a way to hide a misshapen scalp. To the old-fashioned barber, not clever enough to become a "hair stylist," it signaled the end of his profession. I am well aware that for interpreters of all kinds, Freudians most of all, it was an occasion for lengthy, learned expositions. In the grey light of today's world, when economic issues have taken the place of hair, it seems terribly naive to dwell on it. But it would be a terrible mistake to dismiss the subject. Hair, for one thing, grows every day, while the economy stagnates.

I watch the mirror.